# An AMERICAN AWAKENING

## From Ground Zero to Katrina
## The People We Are Free to Be

*To Jason —*
*Whose new friendship is a tremen-*
*dous & life giving gift. So glad to*
*have found a brother who lows*
*truth enough to live it.*

**Courtney Cowart**

*Courtney Cowart*

SEABURY BOOKS
New York

New York cover art courtesy of Shutterstock. New Orleans cover art courtesy of
    Simon Cowart.
Cover design by Simon Cowart
Interior design by Beth Oberholtzer
Photographs by Krystyna Sanderson on photo insert pages 1, 4–8 are from *Light
    at Ground Zero: St. Paul's Chapel After 9/11,* Square Halo Books, Baltimore,
    MD, ISBN 0-9658798-7-9.

Cowart, Courtney.
    An American awakening : from ground zero to Katrina : the people we are
free to be / Courtney Cowart.
    p.    cm.
    ISBN 978-1-59627-101-2 (hardcover w/ jacket)  1. United States—Church
history—21st century.  2. Christian life—United States.  3. Disaster relief—United
States.  4. Suffering—Religious aspects—Christianity.  5. September 11 Terrorist
Attacks, 2001.  6. Hurricane Katrina, 2005.  I. Title.
BR526.C665   2008
277.3'083—dc22
                                                                    2008022469

Seabury Books
445 Fifth Avenue
New York, New York 10016
Seabury Books is an imprint of Church Publishing Incorporated.
www.churchpublishing.org
5 4 3 2 1

*For Katie, Ben, Simon, Gabe, Casey, Pam,*
*Shedrick, Ellene, and Katherine and*
*the whole 9/11 generation of young Americans*
*who are building a new New Orleans and*
*awakening compassion and hope across our land.*

*And for*
*Charles Jenkins*
*Our Leader*

# CONTENTS

# PREFACE

IN THE PAST SEVEN YEARS TWO DEFINING EVENTS HAVE TRANSPIRED ON U.S. soil that have caused Americans in massive numbers to converge spontaneously. The first great birth of unifying empathy, the inauguration of the awakening of which I write, came to us in a rush on the morning of September 11, 2001. This awakening of heart and consciousness did not flicker for a moment and then die. It was sustained by thousands of American volunteers in support of tens of thousands of skilled American laborers and continued without ceasing for a year.

A second great convergence began to move toward the mouth of the mighty Mississippi in the days following Hurricane Katrina on August 29, 2005. Well over 1.1 million Americans have joined this sustained pilgrimage to the City that Care Forgot, in a spirit of repentance, of sacrifice and shared fate with those brought low. This river of civic virtue, the greatest voluntary outpouring of humanity by grassroots white America toward grassroots black America in the history of our nation, continues to flow unabated to this day.

I have stood at the epicenter of the convergence of our people twice in short succession, serving first at Ground Zero and then in Louisiana. Living through these experiences I have come to believe that these two great national mobilizations are signs. In them I believe we have been shown who Americans are free to be.

This book is about that new American identity and the perfecting of our union as citizens of this country. Its sightline is quite different from that of the usual sociologist or cultural critic conducting a national culture scan. Such writers tend to travel widely or to inhabit professional perches that provide wide-angle views.

Mine is a different approach to feeling the pulse of America. It comes from living in the strange and beautiful vortex of post-catastrophic community: dense civilizations that form when a vast sampling of Americans follow their hearts to a point of great need and recombine to create communities of healing. In this story the heartbeat of our nation is measured as it beat within the recovery community at Ground Zero, and as it beats in the most impoverished of New Orleans. It gauges who we are at our spiritual core.

As it is impossible to live immersed in such communities without being transformed, it is also a story about conversion of life: the long journey away from selfishness and greed, as Karen Armstrong has written, and toward greater and greater compassion.

The cultural scanners are predicting the imminent breaking forth of a new American consciousness. This book adds evidence to that claim. Come inside the hearts and minds of our people beginning on the day of 9/11, and feel the process of amendment of life we undergo out of love for each other and in the hope of the new America to be born.

# ACKNOWLEDGMENTS

OF THE MANY LIFE ENDEAVORS THAT HIGHLIGHT VIVIDLY WHAT WE owe to one another, authoring and publishing a book is certainly one. The people who have lived with me through the years chronicled in these pages have enriched my life immeasurably and made this story what it is.

Of my colleagues in New Orleans, I would first like to thank the Right Reverend Charles Jenkins, Episcopal Bishop of the Diocese of Louisiana, for his great kindness in allowing me the time to write this even with so much urgent need still weighing on us in Louisiana. The courageous example of the bishop's wife, Louise Jenkins, has been an inspiration to me and to many, and has helped shape the telling of this story. In addition to them, I would especially like to express my deep appreciation to my colleague Abagail Nelson, of Episcopal Relief and Development (ERD), and all the people of our country who have supported the Gulf Coast ministries financially through ERD.

I thank Shakoor Aljuwani, Nell Bolton, Dana Land, Mark Stevenson, Kenn Elder, Anthony Johnson, Elizabeth Brady, Billie Barbier, Betty Evans, Agatha Townsend, Harriet Murrell, Saundra Reed, Kysha Brown, Dorian Hastings, Shedrick White, Tracie Washington, Gabe Barry, and Casey Leigh, for shouldering extra responsibilities so cheerfully during the writing of this book, and for extending many kindnesses. Collectively these and all my New Orleans colleagues have blessed me with an experience of collegiality and shared commitment that many search their whole lives to find.

The core message of this book comes out of oral histories recorded at Ground Zero after 9/11 and in New Orleans after Katrina. My gratitude extends to all who relived the pain of their experiences in order to tell also about the conversion of life they have received in the midst of so much loss and grief. Without the support of Gary Malkin, the Templeton Foundation's Institute for Research on Unlimited Love, and Dr. Stephen Post, the majority of the Ground Zero recordings would not exist. I would also like to thank Kirstin Paisley, one of the many selfless volunteers who have come to help us in New Orleans, and who conducted many of the Katrina interviews, for her invaluable assistance.

The photographs that immensely enrich this text are treasures to those of us who have lived through these experiences. My appreciation goes out to Krystyna Sanderson, our dear friend and colleague at St. Paul's Chapel, who generously shared work from her own beautiful book of photographs and prayers, *Light at Ground Zero*, and to Jim Belfon, founder of the Gulf South Photography Project for the incredible job he has done of documenting so many aspects of the recovery from Katrina. For all the footwork involved in culling specific images from thousands of photos in our Katrina files, I owe great thanks to Heather Parker.

An abundance of extraordinary mentors have guided me along the path to produce this story and helped turn my yearning to write into a published book. My deepest appreciation is extended to Tom Blackmon, Carl Sword, Fred Burnham, Don Cutler, Jerome Berryman, Bill Kramer and Dennis McManis, whose superb advice and outpouring of practical assistance have been instrumental in achieving this. Davis Perkins, my editor and publisher, belongs in a category of his own. My gratitude to him for giving me the opportunity to voice our story, and for his trust and willingness to take a risk on an ambitious production schedule with a totally unknown writer, is huge. The entire Church Publishing crew—Mark, Jeff, Steve, Ryan, Susie—have shown a passion for the message of this book and a commitment to its excellence that have made them a writer's dream team.

The support of family and friends has buoyed me through some very long days and nights of intense writing and extended hibernation. I would especially like to thank my mother, Ramona O'Neill, and my father, Lawrence Cowart, for the many sacrifices they have made that enabled me to achieve this. And to my stepmother Kathleen Boylan Cowart, I also owe a special debt of gratitude for sharing with me the culture of her native city of New Orleans and her many friends and family there.

Finally, there are the friends who have cheered me on, read pages and pages of drafts, listened to me talk out chapters, and been my sounding board for months on end: Debbie Shew, Peter Grandell, Anna Tonarely, Tom Blackmon, Simon Cowart, Katherine Avery, Martin Cowart, and above all Shakoor Aljuwani. Without these friendships I would never have made it through.

I celebrate the completion of this work as our joint accomplishment. Thanks to all!

## PART 1

# THE SCHOOL OF DEATH

# CHAPTER 1

# ASH TUESDAY

AT 6:00 A.M. I OPEN MY EYES IN A FAIRYTALE BED: A CURVACEOUS nineteenth-century Second Empire sleigh, drawn by carved swans keeping watch over me by night. I am in a graceful chamber adorned with beautiful woodwork that looks like icing on an elaborate white wedding cake. These beaux-arts trimmings were disassembled in Paris and transported to Manhattan in 1902 by the Singer family of sewing-machine fame. Their grand reception hall is now my home, one dreamy room my friends call "Villa Foyer."

The habitat suits me. It is a sanctuary that resonates with my inner world. My field is church history, specifically the history and theology of the Victorian era, that time when feeling, heroism, and the exotic were all the rage. I spend hours in here steeping myself in brittle diaries and musty letters written by inspired nineteenth-century clerics and genteel Anglican ladies yearning for release from lives prescribed and staid.

I also work for Trinity Church, the original Anglican parish in New York, established by royal charter and a gift of land from King William II in 1696. Today this land, increased by another 250 acres from Queen Anne in 1705, makes my employer, a single congregation, the third largest landowner in Manhattan. Three hundred years of accumulated wealth have built a spiritual empire. My office in "Grants" looks down from the height of a modern tower onto the elaborate gothic church built by Richard Upjohn in 1848 at the intersection of

Wall Street and Broadway. This church, the third edifice, was built by some of the nineteenth-century New Yorkers whose letters and diaries I read. Their tombstones dot the landscape surrounding church's graveyard.

By night I research Victorian texts concerned with the squalor of the poor and the rise of industrial slums. I hunt for clues of how those that professed the faith found the courage to enter Dickensian dens of crime and disease and toil for something better. By day I make grants to hone the art of teaching spiritual formation. I identify practices people like me can adopt to receive courage and faith.

I also make grants to champions of social justice working in the Burroughs of New York. The question that fascinates me, day and night, has to do with the factors, aided by grace, that have the power to make people less oblivious and more likely to do something brave. I do this work, however, from an extremely comfortable and decidedly unsqualid perch. I am very afraid of suffering.

Today is slated to bring all of this together. It is a big day in my life and the life of Trinity Church, which is why I wake up so early. It culminates months of effort. At 8:45 a.m. the Archbishop of Wales and twenty-five unusually gifted scholars, monks, priests, and activists are gathering to make a film on "The Shaping of Holy Lives." I need to get moving, as I am hosting the group, but first must center spiritually. It is impossible to talk about holiness if you aren't in touch with its source.

My bare foot emerges from linen sheets and touches the cool glassy surface of a mosaic marble floor. I sit for a few minutes—cozy, secure, happy—light a candle and say my morning prayers. I thank God for the gift of this day, and the opportunity to spend it, miraculously, in the company—all at once and in one place—of almost every person I love and admire most in my field. I bring each person to mind and rest in a sense of gratitude and wonder for their existence, thankful for the privilege of even knowing them. It feels overwhelming, humbling, to acknowledge such an abundance of goodness and grace in the lives of people I am fortunate to call dear friends.

There is Rowan, the archbishop whose writings have shaped my life. There is Peter, the gifted liturgist of the Washington National Cathedral and my dearest friend from seminary. There is Douglas, a Benedictine monk, who, as my spiritual director, has listened to my most private and gut-wrenching confessions for a decade. His face is like the face of Christ to me. There is Elisabeth, my saintly mentor, who has shepherded me through struggles to complete both my master's degree and my doctoral degree. There is Jerome, my first grantee, celebrated around the world for the brilliant formation tools he has developed for children. There is Fred, my colleague at Trinity who has been a great companion to me at work. This day is our joint creation and I know he is as thrilled by the prospect of what we have in store as am I. There are these and twenty others just as singular and special, and I still can't believe I will see them all today.

I ask for grace for us to live up to the promise of the moment. I pray for the stamina to steward the day's demands. I pray that the film we produce will be an instrument of God's purpose and a tool for enriching lives.

All the while it is more difficult than usual to still and focus my spirit this morning. My heart is pounding in anticipation of what lies ahead. I find I can't stay in the present. I can only pray for what this day is about. When I try to detach from my preoccupations and say intercessions for family, for the world and those dying, lost, and in need, I am unsuccessful. They don't seem so important today. I can catch up on the rest of the world tomorrow.

I climb into the shower rehearsing the morning's itinerary in my mind. I must arrive at the office at 8:30. The Archbishop of Wales will be arriving then. The Most Reverend Rowan D. Williams has flown overnight from the West Bank in Palestine through Amsterdam to be with us. Everything must be just so. Traffic can be snarled during the morning rush. Our office tower is next door to the American Stock Exchange and a block and a half from the vortex of the World Trade Center compound. Over three hundred thousand people converge on this, the largest financial capital in the world, each morning. I do not want to be late.

The Director of Trinity Institute, the Reverend Dr. Frederic Burnham, will brief Rowan on the twenty-first floor, while I welcome the other guests in the parlor on the second floor. We will have a civilizing cup of tea and a breakfast bun in the parlor at 8:45. We will move from the parlor and take our places in the church's television studio on the fourth floor of Trinity's vaulting skyscraper at 9:15. The remainder of the day will be spent listening prayerfully to each of the Archbishop's reflections. Following each of these, our studio audience of spiritual practitioners will respond. The whole enterprise will be taped and distributed nationally by Trinity Television. Burt Medley, head of the TV department, will take care of technical details. At noon, during the lunch break I will interview Rowan for "Faces on Faith" in anticipation of the fact that the Queen of England is likely to appoint him to the second most powerful position in the British government, Archbishop of Canterbury, within the year.

My mind turns to sartorial matters. We've been told what the camera likes and dislikes: no clerical collars, no prints, no white shirts. I pluck a royal blue raw silk tunic from my closet, step into my favorite black suede Manolo heels, and rummage for pearls in my jewelry box. This is a morning to take extra care blowing my Manhattan bob to a perfect coif. No sweaty subway-ride to Wall Street. We'll hail a cab on Fifth Avenue and glide down the FDR Drive to our final destination in the shadow of One World Trade. Peter, the canon from the National Cathedral, who arrived from Washington last night, emerges from his morning oblutions downstairs disguised in navy blazer and Charvet tie. We're out the door with time to spare.

What a beautiful day it is. The sunlight bouncing off the river is so brilliant it blinds my eyes. I squeeze Peter's hand to share the thrill in my heart. I picture again each person who is coming. They are all exquisitely dear to me. I truly believe what I have written about this group:

> These are the inspired people, who are concerned with spiritual practice, who open themselves to new experience, and who give of themselves in ways that are transparent to the Divine, who strengthen the spiritual reality of the church and the world, and whose witness directly influences the spiritual formation of others.

I think, what will come of such a day? Something to be cherished; something we will remember forever.

The taxi pulls up to 74 Trinity Place at 8:35. I wave to George the doorman and flash a gigantic grin as we hop into the elevator. On our heels the guests arrive. It feels like a reunion. Our last meeting in March was in the Connecticut countryside. I smile to myself as I recall how we were buried in a blizzard that dumped four feet of snow on the East, completely shutting us in. It was the first time many had met, but we bonded, praying and laughing and playing together in the snow. We stayed up late discussing the contours of a visionary idea: "A New Church for a New World," the cornerstone of which we thought we might call "The Spiritually Illuminating Parish." How can churches in our postmodern context be renewed and become places that truly enlighten, transforming the way we see one another and the way we act in the world? We passionately debated the topic and had a fantastic time.

I am thinking all this as guests are arriving in ones and twos. We are hugging and greeting in that animated way people do if they are genuinely happy to meet. The first impact does not silence our chatter. Our absorption in one other makes us unaware at first. But then someone notices that the light through the windows has changed. It was so sunny but now it is suddenly gray. That observation draws us to a glass wall of windows running the length of the room. We gather. We peer. We frown. Puzzled. What is flying past the windows? What on earth could this be?

Security personnel rush to where we are standing. Outside the parlor is an open-air bridge with a perfect view of the World Trade Center site. The arrival of security makes us anxious. Peter follows them onto the bridge. He looks up the street at the South Tower, as yet still intact. I am looking through the windows at a blizzard of white. I think Connecticut.

But this is not snow it is paper. I squint and look closer. It's on fire. Then I think with some annoyance, who's pouring burning garbage off the roof? But it isn't coming from above. It's defying gravity and zooming sideways. This makes no sense.

Security is on the bridge with walkie-talkies. Was it a bomb? I hear it's a plane—a small plane. Peter comes in and takes me by the hand. He walks me onto the bridge and points down. A pale blue inflatable U-shaped pillow is lying on the walkway. It is charred black. Below I see something spread on the asphalt that I don't want to comprehend and quickly look away.

The air is a blizzard of burning paper and flying grit by now. We are witnessing the contents of the North Tower spewing through a four-story wound between its ninety-fourth and ninety-eighth floors. The gash is from the impact of a Boeing 767, American Airlines Flight 11. The plane has been flown from the Hudson River into the building by Mohammad Atta. The inconceivable has happened blocks from where we stand.

Elisabeth Koenig, my former professor, is tugging at my arm, "I need a phone. Where is a phone?" I walk her into the cafeteria kitchen and point to one mounted on the wall. I walk out to the hall. Mary

Haddad, a former student of mine, is exiting the stairs. She grabs my arm and looks at me wild-eyed. "I saw it. I saw it go in. The plane. Like silver stars. It was beautiful. And then it was hideous." She squeezes me harder. "Horrible. Horrible." I walk her back to the parlor.

Debbie Little, founder of a church comprising the homeless of Boston, says, "I think we should pray." We all form a circle and join hands, but before Debbie can speak a sound rocks the building. It is 9:02. The second plane, another Boeing 767, has approached from the south, flying at nearly 590 mph, and dived into One World Trade, even closer to where we are standing. This time the sound of the explosion and its impact are alarming. We look at each other and know this cannot be an accident.

I am back at the windows looking at Broadway across the Canyon of Heroes. This is the route of the tickertape parades. I am thinking of one last year when the Yankees won the World Series. The bands and all the service people parading up Broadway, everyone cheering and throwing kisses to each other from the windows through the air.

More paper. Total white out. I feel my brain straining furiously. It still won't make sense of what I'm seeing. How could it? I am witnessing the contents of an *8.6 million square foot* structure blow past me.

The guards come in and tell us they are taking us upstairs to the television studio where there are no windows. We obey. I walk down a narrow hall outside a wall of studio monitors. Archbishop Rowan is looking through the glass at the TVs. Our eyes meet in an expression of shared helpless shock and we say nothing. A prayer goes up: Rowan is alive. I stand next to him and stare at the images on the screens. Like last fall's parade, people are hanging out of windows, this time ripping off clothes. Instead of marching bands, battalions of uniformed first-responders stream up Broadway.

Burt Medley tells us to go into the studio and sit in the chairs arranged on a dais. The crew is setting up a big television in the room. We watch dumbfounded. Our camera crew rushes into the room breathless. They have come from the site and have footage of the second plane going in.

I walk to a phone and dial my mother. Her voicemail answers, "Mother, I am in the office at Trinity. We are all here. Rowan is here. We are okay. I wanted you to know that. I love you. I will call you again as soon as I can. Bye." I dial my father, "Daddy, we're in the building at Trinity. They are holding us in the television studio. Don't worry. I'm okay. I'll call you when I can. Please try to call Mother. I couldn't reach her either. I love you. Bye."

By the time I return to the studio we are hearing reports that planes are attacking buildings across the country. The Pentagon has been hit. They are headed for the Capitol, the White House, perhaps the Sears Tower.

Rowan suggests that we pray. The TV volume is muted and he begins with words I will never forget, "We are free to bring our fear before God."

My eyes are shut tight, but I begin to hear the sounds: painful wounded whimpers, half-stifled sobs. Something huge wells up inside me and hot tears wash down my face. I hear those suffering sounds in the silence, the first stillness, and Rowan's words of permission unlock something. The word *vulnerability* does not begin to describe the sensation when I let my defenses go. It feels like infinite falling. Vertigo. It happens on the word *free*.

People are beginning to break down. Rowan prays for the lives of those who were lost, their families, the people on the planes, the pilots, and for the terrorists. He prays for the country and the world. He asks that we be given the grace to help others and to do whatever it is we are called to do in the coming hours, acknowledging this may include our deaths.

It is freezing. I think they've cooled the room to a subzero temperature to compensate for the heat of the studio lights. Or maybe I am going into shock.

The rector of Trinity appears and is trying to say something meaningful and reassuring, and in the middle of a sentence it happens. It is ten minutes after the Pentagon report, and about fifteen minutes after leaving messages for my parents that I am in the office and safe. 9:50 a.m.

Suddenly, it sounds and feels like a hundred bombs are dropping on us as fast as machine gun fire—each one an ear-shattering percussive impact. The whole building is trembling. The lights and the televisions are knocked out, and I can hear the thud of bodies being thrown from chairs to the floor. I am gripping mine for dear life. In the pitch black I hear myself yell out, "Do you smell it? Can you smell it?" An acrid chemical odor overwhelms the room. I choke on my words because there isn't air anymore. Only particles. Dry fuzzy balls and metal flakes with fine dust in between packed so tight there is no oxygen. This is filling my nostrils. I can't suck air through. It is filling my mouth. I can taste burning steel. I can't open my eyes. They are burning too. And then the lights are on and the rector is gone and half of us are on the floor, and we have no idea what that was. But the air is a sea of gray stuff and smoke and the techies say, "We gotta get out of here."

For the first time I think I am going to die. I look from face to face and have a strange reaction, "This is a good death."

I hear people nearby calling out, "Evacuate!" We move toward a concrete stairwell. It's packed with employees. Below I hear someone yell, "Don't come down. It's worse down here!" Above comes the response, "We've got to go down. We're suffocating."

We are on the stairs now. All 250 employees are in here too. Fred Burnham says, "This is getting so bad, at most we have another fifteen minutes." We glance down. Elizabeth Koenig is sitting on the floor with her back against the wall, eyes closed. She is praying. She stands and looks at Rowan. "There is no one I would rather die with than you." Inside I agree. This is why there is peace. We love one another and we are not alone.

Several floors down crowds are filing through a metal fire door. As I move through I stick my yellow legal pad in the door in case it locks behind us and we need to go back. I emerge into the Trinity Day Care Center, and its rainbow of finger-painted artwork and toys and baby cribs. These emblems of innocence juxtaposed with terror are surreal. People are coddling children and trying to seem encouraging and calm. The toddlers are totally brave. Not a single cry. I hear a little girl reassuring her teacher in a baby voice that it's all going to be okay.

They are taking the children into another stairwell ahead of us, and directing us into a concrete emergency exit. I have no idea where I am at this point. Stuart Hoke, the rector's assistant, comes through a door. He is covered in ash and says he has come from the site. The South Tower has collapsed. We are speechless. It has what? Is the whole of Lower Manhattan on fire? I now realize what I believed to be bombs were the floors of the South Tower pancaking as it collapsed. I don't want to think about what I've been inhaling.

There are the tens of thousands of liters of jet fuel that have been released, lead, dioxins, polycelic hydrocarbons, and volatile organic compounds. The particles are a highly alkaline mix of concrete, glass, plastic, paper, the pulverized contents of the Tower and other building materials. Maybe that is why this ash that is caked on our clothes and skin, in our mouths and our hair, stings like hell.

Someone begins passing wet baby bibs down the stairs for us to put over our faces. There is a bald man I don't recognize standing to my left. I politely introduce myself and say, "I don't believe we've met." The sentence sounds absurd once I speak it, but connection and bonding, even with strangers, seems all-important. I want him to know he is not alone and feel he is one of us. It turns out he has come from the tower. He walked toward the church just before it came down. Somehow he wound up down here.

I turn to Fred and Rowan. We have to make a plan. Where do we go when we leave? My mind is picturing an apocalypse outside. I realize poor Rowan has no idea where he is. How terrifying. At least I know the terrain. It hits me I must keep our group together or out-of-towners could get lost. "Fred, do we go north and west to the seminary? Do we go south and east to the Drive?" Will we have to fight our way through fires?

Stuart says it's a total disaster. "You can't see. You can't breathe. You can't go out." But a deep voice at the head of the stairs is booming, "Get out. Get out of the building now! Go, go, GO!"

I reach out and put my arms around two women, Ann and Jennifer. I intensely wish my arms could wrap themselves around all of us. I feel an instinct to herd this flock to safety and think a chilling thought: You brought them here. You're responsible. But I only say out loud, "Okay everyone. Get ready. We're about to see this for the first time."

When I step through the door into Greenwich Street it is not at all what I expect. In my mind's eye the landscape will be red, orange, and black. We will be moving through an inferno. All of Lower Manhattan will look like a cave of hot burning coals. There may be corpses. I have braced myself to see this. But this is not what I see.

In actuality much is incinerated. Sidewalks, streets, cars, windows, ledges are deep in lavender-grey ash. The crystalline blue sky of the early morning is bruised, purple-green. The smoke in the sky continues to partially obscure the sun. It strikes me how unnatural this painter's palette is. The colors are wrong; deeply unsettling. It feels like an alien planet, or passing through to some nightmare parallel universe.

Inside the building the passage of time, the quality of sound, and the sensation of movement seemed normal. But outside everything takes on a hallucinatory quality. Time warps. My limbs are heavy. Walking feels like moving under water. Sound comes at me through a tunnel. Perception is delayed and disjointed. I hear slow gasps. One person says, "Mount St. Helen." Another says, "Nuclear winter." We can only speak impressionistically. We can only think in one or two word fragments.

I expect throngs of screaming, wailing people. Instead there is an eerie vacancy and stillness. Signs of an earlier stampede lay scattered on the street. I stare at thousands of shoes, a thousand neckties, satchels, pocket books, socks. Then there are the office contents: computer monitors blown apart, mangled strands of twisted steel, shattered glass, telephones, Rolodex, file folders, picture frames, notebooks, paperweights—all by the thousands and a good foot or so deep. We are picking our way through it all, but progress is slow. It is difficult to navigate and I am regretting my choice of high heels. But my feet will be sliced to pieces if I dare remove them.

There is one man on the street barking at us. He is not in slow-mo. His voice is fast and jarring. It is blaring in my ear. "Go south. Go south. Go as fast you can. Go faster! Go faster!" He is *screaming*, "Go faster!" I am too fragile to take it. It hurts.

I turn to him with tears in my eyes.

"Why do we have to go faster?"

He says, "Lady, when that second tower comes down you'll know why." Minutes later everything starts to shake.

I reach out for Peter. "I need to hold your hand."

He reaches back. "Don't worry. I know exactly what to do. My mother has been preparing me for this moment my entire life." And then we run, hand in hand, like Peter's mother, Rutta, fled as a girl on the day of the Communist invasion of Riga.

The next part is all confusion. Bits of memory are blacking out. Some of the pieces I have don't fit. I am in one block and then I am in another. I have no recollection of the ones in between. I see no one. I see certain people I know running. I see a woman with a twisted leg being carried by two people, one on either side, and I think, "That is beautiful." Then suddenly I see thousands of people. All converging. They are racing from the direction of the site. There is no sound. Then there is. People are screaming, "Here it comes. Oh my God, here it comes." My back is to the tower. I see Lyndon Harris carrying a child. I see Rowan's stricken face. I see a woman frozen in her tracks, paralyzed with fear, sobbing and shaking uncontrollably. She is wearing a pink sweater and has dirty blond hair. I throw my arm around her.

"Are you alone?" She can only nod. "No you're not! Come with us." I scoop her toward the façade of the building we are approaching. Elizabeth is to my left. Peter is behind me. Rowan and Fred are in front of me. Douglas is close. I've lost track of everyone else.

I am thinking, "Stay together. Stay together." I am willing it with all my might. I am thinking (or am I saying, I can't tell which), "Don't get on the ferry." I have no intention of boarding a boat and evacuating Manhattan Island. It is a long walk to my apartment but perfectly feasible. I will not be herded and neither will my people—not if I can help it.

Now the sound hammers on my brain. It is coming from the sky and from the ground. Above the decibels are so high the air is crackling. Below the ground is roaring and writhing like some mythical savage beast. The sound is bewildering because it is two noises coming from two directions. It feels like it might swallow us.

We are alongside the wall of a building. The stone battlement for some reason feels like a source of protection or security, but I don't know why. It is not obstructing the path of the cloud. The black cloud is coming nearer. I'm not looking. I'm too afraid to look but I sense that it is imminent. Peter is behind me. I want to look at him, but I would have to look at *it*. I sense that he has stopped running. I feel the stampede getting closer. My mind is racing. I am thinking, "What is coming at me? What can I do to protect myself?" And then I think, "There is nothing you can do."

That's when I turn and I face it.

I see it barreling toward me 1,368 feet high. My mind is almost paralyzed, but not quite. I think in milliseconds. I think, "When it gets to me I'll die or live. I have time for one more thought."

It is not exactly a thought. In fact, it feels more like an act. And I can't tell whether I choose it or something is directing me or if it is pure instinct. It seems like all the above at once. With every drop of being I inhale and summon all the life within me. Then, I release it, screaming in my head, "Take me!" It is a thorough and wrenching and absolutely terrifying act. *Surrender* isn't right. It sounds too nice. But there are aspects of the experience that are like that. It is definitely an emptying. The Greek term that theologians use is *kenosis*. But this is a desperately urgent and insistent giving over to God, not at all passive—almost violent. My whole being in a state of utter tremulous powerlessness and fear is pleading for a swift and immediate release from beyond.

Miraculously, it comes. I literally feel the life force inside me starting at my toes and rising up through my spine go out of the top of my head and rocket for somewhere and Someone. I don't know where it is going but it does. There is not a shred of hesitation. It is a *huge rush*—the strangest sensation I have ever experienced *by far*.

All this happens as the black cloud engulfs me and everything around me disappears.

I think, "Now I know. This is how life ends."

But it is not the end. It is the moment I am set free.

## CHAPTER 2

# THE LITTLE CHAPEL
# THAT STOOD

ON SEPTEMBER 16, THE SUNDAY AFTER ASH TUESDAY, I CHOOSE TO GO
back down.

Our buildings—the mother church at the head of Wall Street, our
historic chapel, St. Paul's, across from Building Five, our office tower
just south of the intersection of Liberty and Church—all lie within the
locked down Red Zone the military has occupied since Tuesday night.
Our church's world is in disarray. The institution is paralyzed. Still, in
a small way the faithful remnant will gather.

There is the pride of continuity. In 304 years Trinity has never failed
to conduct Sunday worship somewhere—not through the Revolution,
not through the Civil War, not now. A service is set for three o'clock in
a borrowed Roman Catholic chapel.

For five days I've fielded calls by the hundreds. Each one is a humbling emotional experience, as people I never dreamed would call to
express their grave concern for my safety and gratitude for my life. This
makes my sense of duty to use that life to some immediate, useful purpose increasingly acute. How do I say a cosmic thank you for my life?

I have no idea. But a kind of mantra is needling me. It runs in my
head, as it has since the attack, and it goes something like this: "Only

people, only people, only people matter." I hear it in the shower. I hear it when I am staring at the ceiling unable to sleep. I hear it when I am trying to make myself eat. I hear it when I am trying to pray. I hear it like a voiceover soundtrack even when I'm talking on the phone. I am not sure what it means, but this is new.

Now I walk toward the subway on 78th Street marching to the mantra's rhythm. In my mind I think to myself, "I am going to meet the challenge." I interpret that to mean "introduce yourself again to the present ordeal." What it's all about is to be met and deciphered downtown.

Down the steps I go. I'm holding onto my chant, praying for an uneventful ride, but that is not what I get.

The subway car I enter is seething. On one side of the car, sits a skinny wizened old Sikh in an elaborate gray silk turban clasped in the middle with a Gurmukhi pin. His skin is deeply tanned. He is alone on the bench to my left, sitting very straight and still, with tears pouring silently down his ancient face.

On the other side of the car every seat is taken. All the passengers are packed together like sardines glaring at him with narrow eyes. No one will sit next to him.

Standing at the foot of the car I feel his pain. I stagger toward him as the car rocks and lurches. Then I plant my rear on the bench next to him with a decisive and ungraceful thud. Now everyone is glaring at us both.

We rock along for a couple of stops. It takes emotional energy just to sit there. I'm trying not to glare back.

Suddenly the Sikh stands up and crosses the aisle. He takes a position near one of the doors, standing over a Hispanic mother holding a small infant. His new proximity causes people to flinch. He takes his right hand and reaches into his back pocket. There's a collective protective gasp. Muscles clench in a man a few seats down. He looks like he is poised to pounce.

The Sikh, beaming through his tear-streaked face draws out a harmless crumpled dollar bill. Then he reaches down and stuffs the dollar into the baby's fist. The mother looks at me with dismay—a huge question mark on her face.

Instinctively I lean out into the aisle, cup my hands around my mouth, and say in a loud stage whisper, "Don't stop him! He *needs* to do this."

The mother frowns and leans forward. "So?" she hesitates before finishing. "We know . . . he is . . . not . . . cruel?"

"Yes!" I answer, nodding vigorously—almost desperately. "So we know he is *not* cruel."

With that the car screeches to a stop. The subway doors open. The Sikh steps out. The doors close. Every person in the car exhales and bursts into tears.

I cannot believe what I have just seen. I am wet with perspiration. One moment the car is full of hate so thick it is hard to sit there. Everyone knows they are punishing this man. They make him suffer and enjoy it. But somewhere deeper than this we are clearly longing for the opposite. With one gesture the Sikh revealed his character and how painfully we misjudged.

"Lord, how we are really longing for kindness," I cry inside. We have seen hatred, now we need to touch something better.

I spend most of my time on my knees in the Shrine of Elizabeth Seton thinking that what occurred on the subway feels more holy than what's happening here. I wonder what our congregation's steps toward mission will be. There are no clues in this service.

Afterwards we divide into groups to check on Trinity's properties. I join the group of three heading for St. Paul's. Everything is strange and new. The streets are swarming with soldiers, Humvees, walls of cops manning barricades that stretch the length of Broadway. Yellow crime-scene tape surrounds the mother church. FBI agents are poring through debris in our cemetery, poking around the tomb of the man on the ten-dollar bill. Above, guards are patrolling rooftops. Thousands of firemen are marching through streets.

These blocks are not what they were last Tuesday. The crowds, the noise, the buzz are, in fact the reverse. Con Edison blue and Verizon orange hardhats vibrate to the sound of jackhammers. The noise is deafening. Fires still rage, but the site is crawling with workers. Impressive cranes tower above, hanging in the sky.

All of this industriousness signals a massive job is underway. Damage to water, gas, electric, and telecommunications is severe. In the collapse steel beams have speared the streets driving to a depth of thirty feet. The entire fiber-optic and electric power grid is destroyed. Water mains and gas lines are crushed. Vehicles of all types are hammered as many as five stories underground. One and a half million tons of debris is piled in a mountain rising fifty to one hundred and fifty feet high.

We reach the chapel. Its dark silhouette, perched on the very precipice of the site, stands apart from the fire's red glare. St. Paul's, the oldest church in continuous use in the city of Manhattan, has stood its ground—genteel as ever—strangely still and totally unmoved. Meanwhile, battalions of workers toil in its shadow.

The chapel was built in 1766 when the port to our south was tiny. St. Paul's was located in the country, set in a pastoral field. Its first rescue occurred in 1776 when the building was threatened by fire. While nearly a quarter of Manhattan was destroyed, a brigade of volunteers saved the chapel. It was considered a miracle that the church survived the surrounding flames. Trinity was not so fortunate. That congregation was not rebuilt for years.

Because citizens united and prevailed, when George Washington was inaugurated at Federal Hall in 1789, as the new Republic's president, it was to St. Paul's that he came to pray. He led a procession, with Congress, up the route I have just traversed. Of the two remaining box pews in St. Paul's, one belongs to Washington from the time of that historic day.

Above Washington's pew hangs one of the earliest paintings of the Great Seal of the United States, commissioned by Trinity's vestry in 1785. In years past I have knelt and gazed at the cryptic symbols crowding the painting's canvas. A message is here in code.

At the center of the painting is the bald American eagle, its wings outstretched. The breast of the bird bears a shield—the country's coat of arms. It is composed of thirteen stripes that represent the states joined into one solid compact. At their head, and joining them, is a horizontal blue band, or "chief" that unites the whole. The stripes depend upon that union and its strength.

In the eagle's right talon, interpreted as its strongest, is an olive branch with thirteen olives representing the original colonies. The eagle's head is turned in this direction, and away from its left. On the weaker side, the left, the talon holds a bundle of arrows. The symbols seem to say the power of peace is stronger and preferred by the eagle to the power of war. Our nation's motto is also expressed by words in the eagle's beak: *E Pluribus Unum*. Out of many, one.

Behind the eagle's head is a constellation of thirteen stars floating in a circle of blue. Rays of golden light surround it. This "glory"—a kind of halo—symbolizes a new state taking its place and rank among the nations. Glory is a symbolic theme that echoes in other parts of St.

Paul's. The ornamental design over the altar is a depiction of glory too. This altarpiece is the work of Pierre L'Enfant, designer of Washington, D.C. Mount Sinai rises in clouds and lightning. It is the *Shekinah* — the spirit, the glory of God that has led the people of God out of bondage. With the name of Yahweh in Hebrew at the pinnacle are the commandments Moses received.

Today the chapel is vacant, menacing. There is no electricity, no water. No one has ascertained if the building is structurally sound, but not a windowpane is cracked. So far the church functions mainly as a warehouse. There is one card table inside the front door with a small collection of sweatshirts and over-the-counter drug store items like eye drops and cough medicine sitting on it. A handful of recovery workers are wandering wearily in and out.

I pass through to the rear of the building. You cannot be closer to Ground Zero than this unless you are standing in it. The churchyard slopes from Broadway down to the eastern perimeter at Church Street and what is left of Building Five. Inside our gates the lawn is horrendous—deep in the detritus of lost lives. FBI is here too—shoveling evidence into bags. An enormous sycamore tree near Church Street is upended. Its dirt-caked root ball pierces the sky. Beyond the ancient cemetery with its eighteenth-century moss-covered tombstones is a new tomb that reaches to the river. In its center the haunting, faintly gothic ruins of the towers form the outlines of a mad cathedral. Underneath the odor from fire is the sickening stench of death.

To my left is the shell of the Millennium Hilton—definitely postmillennial now. The remaining trees above my head are dripping with shredded paper and strips of steel. Above the treetops St. Paul's beautiful but fragile windowed steeple rises miraculously, perfectly intact.

I wander back toward Broadway. It is hard to believe with its location, its uncanny lack of damage, and the thousands of surrounding workers that St. Paul's is not destined for some use. But so far the only real signs of what might be are on the sidewalk. Church volunteers from General Seminary and Seaman's Church Institute have joined forces with local residents and businesses from the neighborhood, firing up grills. Volunteers are feeding the workers by the hundreds, but so far they have not been allowed inside.

On Wednesday I return to St. Paul's for part two of my reconnaissance mission. On Monday Trinity senior staff had been called together at the law offices of Davis Polk. It is our first meeting since the attack. In the discussion a rotation to take shifts at St. Paul's is established. Fred Burnham and I both attend and sign up. So far, however, neither of us has heard a word. We decide to meet at the chapel to ask why.

As we approach we can see Lyndon Harris, priest-in-charge of St. Paul's, standing in the chapel's doorway. Clothed in black clericals and boots, with a respirator dangling from his neck he looks the part of a wounded healer. He is standing alone, his handsome features smeared with black soot. Next to him is one humble, unassuming sign drawn with magic marker on a sheet of white paper. It says, simply, "Enter, Rest, and Pray."

Lyndon confirms that Trinity staff support has not materialized. Fred steps into the breach. "Tonight's my shift. When we've finished here go home and get some rest." Lyndon is tough, but clearly so grateful to Fred he almost cries. He has been through a very rough week. We urge him to spill his guts, just tell us the whole story. We sense he needs a sympathetic ear.

Lyndon begins. "On Wednesday I was really concerned that I get to St. Paul's and figure out what to do. I put the keys to the church in my pocket and started walking downtown. I was certain the church was destroyed but hoping to see what was left, and I wanted to retrieve the Great Seal from the ruins.

"When I got a little north of City Hall I saw the steeple. I just broke into tears. I got out those huge old keys and found the right one. I was freaked out going in alone. It was so eerie.

"When I came out there was a firefighter walking down Broadway. He was exhausted. He'd been working since the attack, and this was twenty-four hours later. He asked if he could come into St. Paul's and take a nap. I told him no, not yet, because I didn't know if the building was safe. I told him people were resting at the Millennium Hilton. That haunts me. He wanted to come into the chapel and I said no."

This is the first of a series of encounters. Lyndon is the lone priest from Trinity walking the pile. On Thursday, when the general belief is that two more skyscrapers will tumble, security bars him from the chapel. Lyndon's attempt to reverse his haunting "No" of the previous day is stymied, so he goes one step further and enters the morgue.

"I bumped into some Roman Catholic priests who invited me to join them in blessing body parts. I said, 'I'm willing,' but I was really scared.

"Father James looked at me—short wiry guy, smokes like a smoke-stack—looks at me and says, 'There's no heroes down here. If you got to vomit, go vomit. Just come back.'

"So I went to the morgue over at the Winter Garden and I was stunned. There were people slogging around, carrying body bags in two or three inches of water.

"So now we're saying blessings over these body bags. The men are coming out of the pile looking so haggard. I've never seen anyone look as bad as these guys. This ladder fireman came out exhausted and con-sumed with grief. They'd been working two days straight, doing their best trying to find the two brothers of one of the guys. One brother was a fireman. The other was a policeman. They were trying frantically to find them. I weep when I think about them—when I see his face."

On Friday Trinity still has not sent structural engineers to ascertain the soundness of the building. Again Lyndon cannot open up. He makes a call and asks directly what he has permission to do. The vicar says he may allow access for prayer.

The responders have been saying every day to Lyndon how much they need the church. "When I'm in the pile with the guys they are say-ing, 'Thank you. Thank you. Thank you for being here. To see a col-lar, to see a cross means the world. It lifts us up and helps us do what we need to do.'" Because of these experiences Lyndon feels he has a new charge. "Those guys are my congregation. I guess I'm a priest of the pile. But what can I do? I don't know . . ."

On Friday night the pressure Lyndon feels inside is mirrored back by people in the street.

"A guy named Roger Bentley and the fellows he's recruited cruised by in their big red truck. Roger gets out of the truck and starts urging me to open the doors to the chapel. I wasn't ugly but I was quite firm. I pulled Roger aside and really got in his face. I told him, 'I more than anybody want to see something happen at St. Paul's, but until I am sure the building is safe, until we have a plan or an idea of what we can do and do well, until I feel certain that what we do can be sustained, I won't open the doors.'

"They sent Julianne Margulies over—the star of *ER*. They sent her over to give me hell too. I said right back to her, 'Until I know the build-ing is safe I'm not opening it.' And she said, 'I'll get you a structural engineer.' And I said, 'I have to have my own.' I knew it wouldn't satisfy Trinity otherwise. But I satisfied her by saying, 'Let's set something up on the sidewalk.'

"We set up grills and began cooking. Then Roger and the guys had a foundry make more yesterday. The new ones cook a hundred burgers at a time. We have about five of them going day and night around the clock. What a joy to flip a burger and put it on a bun. I'm ecstatic. We aren't saving the world but we are doing something.

"Now we are fighting the Health Department. Fred, this is what you need to know tonight. The health department keeps coming by and hassling us. It's really frustrating. There's a woman who keeps coming by and sticking her thermometer in the burgers. It's the one thing we can do to make a difference for these guys.

"To tell you the truth I am at my wits' end. There just doesn't seem to be a lot of interest in this from the higher ups. I'm pretty close to despairing. I feel like I am fighting alone."

My immediate thought is we need more help. We need people with more expertise than we have, and we must take the initiative to find them. Instantly two people spring to my mind. One I know extremely well, and one just barely, but I feel we need them both. I don't give much explanation. I don't give a thought to what Trinity will think. I just tell Lyndon and Fred I'm going to get these people. As Lyndon predicts, on Wednesday night the barbecue on Broadway is shut down. We are back at square one.

I go in search of Martin. He is one I believe can help. My cousin has owned a restaurant a few blocks away, but two weeks ago it closed when Martin lost his lease. We were totally crushed at the time. Martin is unemployed. Now that once sad fact gives me hope.

Martin says, "Yes, but this may be out of my league. How can I possibly? I'm not big enough." We all know how he feels, but we have to start somewhere.

Within a day a small team of friends comes together. We move the food from the sidewalk to our porch. This is St. Paul's property but technically it's not inside. No permission is sought; we just do it.

We push ourselves mercilessly and create a network of New York restaurants that commit to donate and deliver thousands of meals each day. No one we ask says, "No." No one we ask even says, "Maybe." A host of people partner: from security on the perimeter of the Red Zone to get clearance for our deliveries, to Mary Morris at General

Seminary who works with us to send more volunteers, to total strangers who've shown up on our doorstep who say they can get plates, serving utensils, sterno to keep the food hot, and any other supplies we need to do this. The cooperation is immediate, total, and free of charge. It happens so fast it is hard to keep up with the pace. The willingness of people surprises me.

Once we're serving breakfast by the Waldorf, lunch by Zabar's, and dinner by The Cleaver Company and *Le Zie*, the number of workers adopting St. Paul's as their base begins to soar. Again we are taken completely off guard. We buy a clicker and count. Suddenly the daily total coming for meals is averaging three thousand workers a day—and climbing. The only way we can keep on top of it all is to work almost twenty-four hours a day. We come at 4:00 a.m. and stay until 6:00 a.m. the next day. Go home and sleep until 8:00 a.m. and then come back through the night.

Meanwhile the other person I've tracked down is Bethany Ann Putnam. I know her because she has been after us for a grant for several months. I know very little about Bethany, but I do know Labor of Love helps churches in times of disaster. My brief interactions with her so far tell me she is gutsy. I consult with Lyndon and he agrees, "Invite her to New York."

Bethany is found. I ask her to pack her bags in North Carolina and hit the road right away. She says, "This is the answer to so many prayers I can't even begin to tell you. Let me do one batch of laundry then I'll load the trailer and go." Immediately she has something to add. "Courtney, I interviewed a girl named Katherine Avery last Friday. She's in Spartanburg, South Carolina. May I call her and bring her too?" The answer is, "Yes." We are more than eager for help.

Katherine calls me at midnight. She needs to talk out this choice. After all, she explains, "I'm twenty-three, from Spartanburg, and I've never even been to New York City." But I find out Katherine is not a novice when it comes to mission work.

"I did do some work in Jamaica. We were taking care of disabled orphans, and we built a house for Cowie who lived in the garbage dump. That was when I was happiest." A feeling comes over me when I hear her say that. It is not the sort of statement I could ever imagine making myself. This is the kind of person I want to teach me.

"But people are asking," Katherine continues, "'Are you crazy? New Yorkers are fleeing the city!' I feel like I have to surrender every fear, every inhibition to do this. Like Lord, just break me down and build me up again."

By morning Katherine has made the choice each of us has made in different ways. She says, "I am coming, but I am scared to death."

The next day Lyndon asks me to take a walk. This is the invitation I want and dread. I know it means crossing a threshold. In my mind this is the choice to go all the way, leave the comparatively safe periphery and meet the problem we are here to address head on.

We walk to the northwest side of the site and are waved through by the guards. Leaving Vesey Street behind we travel south to the interior. The further we go the more I have the sense of no return. I will not see the heart of this with my own two eyes and come out still the same.

When we reach the center of the pile we stand in the bottom of a jagged bowl—a gray, ashen highway carved deep into the heart of darkness. Lyndon is accustomed, but I am becoming like steel—so tense. I am fighting to fend off whatever this is in here. My soul is flashing warnings. My flesh has become like armor. I wrap my fingers around my cross and squeeze. "No," I am saying to this terrible energy. "No. You cannot have me."

This concentrated force field does not want entry. Its suction is the pull of anti-life. It is sucking at what little left in here is still alive. Even color is drained. "Utter negation of life," I whisper. Lyndon nods, "The wasteland."

The sheer cliffs of the pile rise to the east of where we are standing. These are the sliced corpses of buildings. Their bones are fractured. Their guts are spilling out. Sinews of tangled cable snake through eviscerated black tissue matted in clumps. "Where are we going?" I ask. Lyndon answers, "In there."

We start to walk a slope. I feel extremely weak and horribly insignificant. The bewildering scale and uncountable number of shards, billions of gargantuan matchsticks dropped like giant pick-up sticks pointing in every direction, make me feel like a speck. The thought of any team tackling this is irrational—absurd, pointless, impossible. This is a lost world. I hear the voice of one of the workers, "I looked at it and thought ten years it will take to do this. Ten years! Where do we even begin?"

The supernatural dimension of this place is also giving me the creeps. The voice of another worker comes to me. "I looked into the valley of twisted steel across the entire scene. Then I closed my eyes and went into a trance. All I heard was, 'Aaaah. Aaaah.' Moaning. Wailing. Something. My knees buckled. I almost fell to my knees."

I've never stood directly on ground where people came seeking to obliterate life. Most terrifying is the fact that you can still feel that intention to take, to sever, to confuse, to quell. There is an overwhelming feeling of subtraction. I feel it like hunger in my stomach, a great gnawing, acid emptiness that makes me slightly sick.

All this tempts me to think, "Forget this, you fool. Get out of here now. It is not too late to run."

But this dissipates once we are with the workers. In defiance of death, destruction, fear, and the horrible toll working in here must take on any human are the acts I am about to see.

The man in the hazmat suit, who looks like a yellow astronaut, directs us to where they are digging. A bone, a respirator, and a piece of fireproof garment have been found. This means the remains of a fireman are probably nearby. The team that is searching kneels with four-pronged rakes, sad instruments of love, in hand.

In the intense heat radiating through our clothes the workers gently rake the ash. The smell of decay is strong, but the seekers do not notice. They commune so intently with the one who is lost. I can almost hear them praying, "I will dig on my knees to find you. I will scoop you into my hand. I will carry you out and take you where we can name you. We will find the ones who love you and know that you belong. We did not leave you. We would never leave you in Hell."

I am spellbound. Despite the hideous strength that is palpable, this contrasting commitment is total. It began the morning of the attack. It persisted through the early days and hours of search and rescue. Now it continues as the firefighters I see reach for those they failed to save on 9/11. These are human beings bound to the lost by one absolute and undeterred purpose: to protect, to serve, and to rescue lives—no matter the cost, no matter the grave.

I think of what a firefighter said to me. "See this?" he asked, pointing to the shield in the shape of a Maltese cross stitched on his uniform. "It means that the person who wears this is willing to lay down his life for you." I have never been completely surrounded by the presence of people like this.

The searchers speak in low voices. One of the ones who laid down his life has been found. We gather the person's remains from the ash, immediately encircling the container in a blanket of prayer. One extraordinary life to thank the Creator for making. One life given for this world. One death that makes us incomplete forever. One of us.

The remains of the fireman are transferred now to a red biohazard container, and then to a body bag. I can see a stretcher approaching. It is draped with a flag. The honor guard forms—six pallbearers—three on either side. The signal goes out and all the machinery stops in honor of the solemn ritual now beginning. The honor guards process.

I hear the voice of Tony, a sanitation worker and volunteer fireman.

"I really believe in my heart they knew they weren't coming out. Everybody obviously gave up their life, but the firemen actually gave up their life to save somebody else's, going in knowing full well they weren't coming out. So that is why I don't care what we have to do. It doesn't matter. I don't care if they ask me to get down on one of those streets and lick it with my tongue. It won't bother me. Because you can't put any price on that there—what they did. So whatever it takes . . ."

I look around me at what I see: the enormity of what it means here to commit to "whatever it takes." How different the response of these workers from my paltry initial reaction, how I entered this and felt defeated—wanted to run and hide. Didn't believe we had it in us. But not Tony. Not these guys.

Thank God that seeing humanity loved like this renews the passion to give all you can. Being in the presence of these men I begin to believe just maybe, if something of their commitment to life rubs off on the rest of us, many will be activated to give their all, and we will actually recover this unfathomable wreckage and cherish every identifiable remain. If anything can tap into wells of passion and kindle the "whatever it takes" so that it catches, leaps from person to person, causes a chain reaction, seeing the sacrifices of these responders and remembering how they behaved in the moment of trial—that has the power to do it. I know I've never been so moved. They are bringing something out in me I never knew existed: a fierce desire not to sit on blessings such as these.

How many of us, I wonder, are having this experience in some way, in some measure? If thousands (maybe millions), this must be the most remarkable feature of the days we are living through. I don't know if this is the case, but I feel as though I might be in the grip of a larger initiation.

I catch the parable of the firefighters' task inside this giant wreck. If they represent how far our human hearts can go, our enormous capacity to care, to give, to sacrifice for each other, maybe the pile shows the time has come to unleash this power in all of us.

As if in answer to my doubts and hopes, the very next morning strangers begin to make their calls. The first one comes completely out of the blue.

"Good morning, ma'am?"

"Yes."

"Hello, ma'am. My name is Ann Gates, and I'm calling from Clyde, North Carolina."

"Good morning, Ann."

"Ma'am, we heard about what y'all are doin' up there at the chapel at our Bible meetin' last night, and I'm just callin' to ask if we could send y'all somethin' y'all really need."

"Well, thank you. Thank you so much for asking."

"You know we'd do anythin' for our heroes, ma'am, but we just donnow what they really need."

"Well, I can tell you, Ann. What workers need right now is boots. We've got 2000-degree fires burning, and they're melting the soles off their shoes."

"Ah think ah might just be able to do somethin' about that. Now if we send a trucker, ma'am, do you reckon he'll be able to get through? Anuther church down heah sent some supplies and they got turned back."

"You're right. It happens, but if you get those boots to us I promise you we'll get them to the workers."

"Alright then. Lemme see what ah can do and I'll cawl you back."

"That'd be great, Ann. God bless."

"God bless you, ma'am, and God bless what y'all are doin'."

I hear an engine roar in the background.

"What's that?"

"Sorry, ma'am. I'm on my Harley."

"Well have a nice ride, Ann."

'Sure will. Bye."

A few hours later the phone rings again.

"Hello, ma'am?"

"Yes, hello."

"Ma'am, mah name is Fred Luther. I'm down in North Carolina, and I got some boots here ah'd like to run up there to you."

"Oh my gosh, Fred. That's fantastic!"

"Yep, I got me here eight hundred par, and ah'm fixin' to head on up there. Never been to New York City before. How ah'm gonna fine you?"

"When you think you'll get here, Fred?"

"Well, I reckon it'll take me about fifteen hours. Ah'm gonna drive straight through."

"Okay, Fred. When you get outside New York you just call me, and we'll figure it out from there. I'll meet you or something. Doesn't matter what time it is. You just call me okay?"

"Okay, ma'am. Ah'm on my way."

Hours later the eighteen-wheelers begin to arrive. We don't know who sent them but they deliver supplies by the ton. We unload and cart boxes without ceasing. Still they keep coming. We're drowning in abundance. By nightfall we sense that something bigger is about to hit us. Even so we really cannot conceive of what morning will bring.

The next day the empathy of the world gives birth, and it comes to the site in a rush. That little prayer, "Send me," whispered on the lips of thousands. Hoards of volunteers with no previous ties to the church, from every faith tradition and no faith tradition, begin to appear, as if some invisible homing device in our steeple has signaled to their hearts. Standing at the epicenter and witnessing this changes my view of people forever. Even the street folks of the neighborhood show up in a gang to give us their cups of coins.

There is the elderly African American woman who struggles toward the chapel gates. She says she has come all the way from the Bronx on the subway to give us her cane. It is all she has to give, but she thinks someone is going to hurt himself in the site, and when that person does she wants them to have her cane.

There is a man who comes to the chapel and counts out $10,000 in one hundred dollar bills and leaves refusing to give us his name. There are dozens of children arriving. Moms report they will not rest until their piggy banks are placed in our hands.

There are the Cajun chefs who have collected donations and driven all the way from Louisiana. They are coming straight down Broadway at 2:00 a.m. in a doublewide trailer refitted as a kitchen. They park around the corner on Fulton between Broadway and Church Street, put their rocking chairs and some eight hundred gallon crock-pots in the street. In their overalls and straw hats they will cook Creole delights for a week.

The folks from Maine arrive. They bring hundreds of homemade apple pies, each one in its own pastry box adorned with a painstakingly drawn message to a worker from a child. There is the airfreight delivery overnight of hundreds of pounds of fresh tuna, flats of pineapple, and fresh flower leis from Hawaii.

The banners and letters pour in—the first from the firefighters of Oklahoma City. Flags made out of the hands of thousands of children, flags made out the faces of thousands of people. Hundreds of hours of labor go into making the handmade quilts and huge elaborate paintings that arrive. Many are hand carried from cities around the world.

Multiply these examples by thousands, and then multiply again. The polyphony of response and the magnificent diversity of envoys simply astound us.

The number of new faces who have adopted us as their base to serve the responders is staggering. And it is quite an American cast. Everything from your most staid church ladies to wild-looking teens with tattoos, every sort of New York character from Peter X, whose name is too long to pronounce, to Brooklyn Bridge Lou with his black beard, Old Glory hardhat, and pirate's loop through his ear, to that pair "the Velvet Fog" who appear at dusk and vanish daily at dawn. There are Amish farmers, Mennonites, hip L.A. documentary film makers, Native American chiefs, Tibetan monks, bikers, opera stars, movie stars, even people dressed up posing as firefighters we later find out are imposters. We are mobbed, besieged by their totally unfamiliar, absolutely fantastic, completely overwhelming love.

The church has never given the okay to open the chapel's doors for anything more than prayer. But the people's zeal to serve has blown the doors wide open, and completely burst our hearts. The idea of saying, "No, thank you," is utterly inconceivable. I have never felt such a frenzy of gratitude, such a bond between strangers, or such over-the-top joy. The throng I dimly dared to hope for has come.

Until this moment I've never had the slightest inkling what mainstream Americans are made of. Now I feel affiliated with them. I see strangers in a completely new light, even those I might not have thought too highly of before.

I realize it's taken everything that's happened to me in these past few weeks to make me this receptive and grateful. It took running from the black cloud reaching for strangers, desperately crying inside, "I do not want to see you die! I want you to see you live!" It took seeing this desire to preserve human life spring forth in us all automatically. It took being unbelievably humbled by the need for assistance and just plain kindness, and thousands of strangers bearing help appearing from nowhere. It took seeing the emergency services enduring inhuman pain because their love for human life is beyond the reach of death to deter them. It took being surprised by the Sikh.

I guess I had to be bludgeoned by all these stunning moments of blessing to see how every person matters. How we cannot be what we need to be without that union and strength. Would we ever have opened the chapel fully without this push from outside? Would we have given up fighting, deciding this was too big to sustain? Would we have run out of steam to maintain this crazy pace without the inspiration and assistance of others to invigorate resolve? It has taken repeated blows to my ego and self-preoccupation to strip illusions that would doom the progress to come.

Archbishop Rowan is one who has said that need is the beginning of truthfulness. Need has made me truthful about how partial I am. It's dramatically changed the way I look at strangers. It's painful to admit, but standing in the pile, when I doubted our ability to meet this challenge, deep down I did not believe the average person had very much to offer. Now I am feeling the opposite. What's happened to me in a short span of time has totally rocked my world.

This is completely changing the quality of every moment. Suddenly no one is invisible to me anymore. I actually see everyone, even those I am merely passing in the street. It's because I'm beginning to expect things of people—great things. I have a newfound sense of curiosity about every kind of person.

I'm beginning to want my routine to be disrupted by people I don't know. I'd be disappointed now if a day went by without being surprised by some remarkable quality revealed in somebody new. Apparently, contrary to what I've been taught by much of my life experience, everyone has something to offer the common good. Now I really want to see whatever that might be. And wanting to see it, I do see it—everywhere I turn.

The following day I leave the chapel for home in the late afternoon. I walk wearily to the Wall Street stop and join the throngs squeezing into the subway. I'm planning to kick back and lose myself in all these thoughts and feelings, but once again I enter a car where something important happens.

The train is packed with people. We've all been in the debris-filled air and we all look a little bit grimy. We've tracked the muck from the site onto the subway floor and its greasy coating is on our clothes and our faces.

But there is one family that looks untouched—incredibly pristine and shiny. The mother is very blond and blue-eyed. Her flaxen hair is braided in pigtails tied with powder blue bows. The father is also fair. They look like they might be Nordic. In front of them is their baby, about six months old. He is gurgling in his stroller, swathed in matching powder blue clothes and an adorable blue knit hat.

Across from him and next to me is a tall African American teen. His mane of dreadlocks is tied up in a dramatic do with a shiny black rayon wrapper. The crown gives him the air of an urban warrior. There are numerous scars on his angular face that look like they might have been made by the blade of a knife.

We are all entranced by the baby. The parents are looking a little self-conscious with so much attention from strangers trained on their child. But it's all clearly kind.

Then the youth pipes up. "Hey, mommy."

The woman looks a bit startled.

"Hey, mommy!" the youth says again.

"Yes?" the woman who looks like Heidi replies.

"I really like that baby."

We can't help but smile.

"Isn't he the cutest thing you ever did see?"

Our smiles grow bigger. A few people chuckle. Others nod in agreement. Now we're even more absorbed in admiring this beautiful child.

"You know what I hope for that baby?" the young man continues, addressing all of us. "I'll tell you what I hope. I hope that baby don't know nuthin' 'bout none of this . . . nuthin' cept what he reads in books."

The air in the car grows hushed. You can feel everyone's sadness and longing. We keep staring together in silence. The longer we feel in unison the more it seems the baby actually glows. We can't take our eyes off of him. The innocence, the promise, the hope for a future untainted by violence and death—all directed toward this little life—and given voice by the boy with the terrible scars.

I come up out of the subway onto Lexington, almost home. The newsstand across the street from the subway exit is assembling tomorrow's edition of the *New York Times*. About halfway up the steps my sightline pops above street level. I see the bottom of a wall of newspapers stacked on the sidewalk. The partial image I recognize on the cover makes my eyes lock. One step higher and I can see more. More newspapers, more of the image. I take the next steps two at a time. Now I can see hundreds and hundreds of newspapers—the image repeated hundreds and hundreds of times. I blink my eyes and then I blink again. Yes, it is the chapel. Lifted up for all the world to see.

I speed dial Lyndon and get his voicemail. But as I try to leave a message, I am choked. The intensity of days in the pile, the sense that something enormous and contagious is breaking loose—in the subway, in the streets, in me, and now this, all crash together to create a very large lump in my throat. I am so full I can't get the words out.

———◆———

The chapel now has thousands of folks literally camped on our doorstep. Given my new attitude, I want the people to have this church, to make sure it stays in their hands. Fortunately all of us calling the shots on the ground, winging this daring effort, are of the same mind and spirit. We see St. Paul's as the location thousands of strangers have chosen to entrust with their greatest treasure, what Tony from sanitation calls "that little bit we have inside," our innate appreciation of each other and deep desire to help each other with the problems we face.

So far we have operated intuitively but now we are beginning to agree that we need to be more intentional about assessing what we are doing and what we think it might achieve. It is obvious that we want to serve and support the workers who have unlocked such deep wells of admiration, care, and concern in so many. But there are multiple ways that we could approach doing this.

We agree that we really want to undertake this work in the spirit of the firefighters. We believe this community has been inspired by their example and wants to make the fire department's principle—total passionate, whatever-it-takes concern for human life—our principle and guide for all that we do. We not only want to serve the workers, but we want to serve them in a way that's consistent with the value that has set our hearts on fire.

We can't help but be keenly sensitive to the fact that we are all living and working in a place destroyed by an ethos of violence and hatred where thousands have been killed. You can smell it—all the time. The aroma reminds us what happens when human life has lost its value. When some people have decided that "those people" are nothing.

All of us working together at St. Paul's agree we never want to go back to our dulled, pre-9/11 psyche when it comes to appreciating others. We want to be the opposite of the horrendous destruction staring at us across the street, and move farther and farther away from the possibility of participating in any way with terror's repetition.

Lyndon tells us he passed a sign in the subway that said, "Don't Stop Here." It seemed to him to carry a message for us. We've been cracked open and we are responding, but we must keep going or else we'll close up again. This is what we sense intuitively.

We believe the most important ingredient if we want to achieve these deep desires is that every person who enters St. Paul's must know they are highly and equally valued. It's not enough for a few to feel it for a time and then go back to the status quo. Everyone must feel it from everyone else constantly so that the imprint of this experience becomes indelible.

We begin to think about how you ensure that the ethos of the chapel reinforces that message in everything and everyone. One would think this would be automatic for the church, but it is not in the habit of old institutions to do this naturally. They too, like people, must be re-created.

We agree the space seems chosen for something truly unknown—the enactment of a civic mystery. God is certainly present in this, but it goes way beyond the usual contours of institutional religion. There is no blueprint we know for a post-catastrophic, ecclesial rebirth such as this. We will draw some outlines, and the American people who've claimed the church will color them in with all their wisdom, love, and caring. The whole of the chapel should be a work of the American people— their offering to God and to one another in this time of redefinition. It is beyond any of us to prophesy what this work will look like in its full fruition. As Lyndon says, the main character here is the Spirit, and the rest of us are honored to be bit players invited along for the ride.

In the dark of night I sit with Bethany in an open gallery that looks over the ground floor of the chapel. This gives us a bird's eye view of the comings and goings beneath. We have spiral notebooks in our laps and are studying the rhythms and movement of the people moving in and out. I can see the wheels turning furiously in Bethany's mind. She is imagining with all her might, creating the contours *ex nihilo*, drawing maps, and making lists of names. An altruistic architect, she is designing the skeletal structure, using the resources that have come into our hands.

These include not only a staggering, eccentric array of supplies and all sorts of letters and artwork, but also the panoply of human gifts and skills. Keeping the workers' needs always in the forefront of her thoughts, she is matching resources with very specific kinds of pain the responders endure daily: in mind, body, and spirit. I realize when we pack all of this into one enormous two-story room the density will be stunning. I find myself living in a state of suspense anticipating a remarkable outcome.

About midnight, at Bethany's suggestion we begin mounting letters and cards. Volunteers climb ladders carrying tacks and tape. The pink walls of the chapel vanish behind a rainbow of children's love. Every inch of interior space is covered since we display it all. Floor to ceiling is papered as letters come out of their boxes. Each one is a unique delight. We ask, "Where should this precious one be hung?" It feels like a spectacular tree-trimming night. Hundreds of people are helping.

All the letters express support, regard, and thanks to the workers in ways grown-ups never would. Lyndon finds one from a little girl and her dog, signed with a smeared paw print. "Looks like there was a struggle," Lyndon says with a grin. Katherine's favorite has a drawing of a bulbous purple plane approaching a really tall skinny very crooked green tower. Below there's a teeny little stick figure on the ground. He says prophetically, "I smell trubble."

My favorite is the one from Claudia Fischer who lives in Scarsdale, New York. It captures perfectly the sentiment that has united all these thousands of people.

Dear firefighter,

There are many deaths that I can die. Cancer, heart attack, AIDS, hepatitis, sickle cell anemia, leukemia, natural causes, choking, being strangled, shot, or hanged. I could get the death penalty or rabies, or a snakebite, or a wild animal could attack me. I could get run over by a car, be in a car crash, fall, slip, get a concussion, get smallpox or be stabbed, crack my skull, get poisoned, heart disease, get stung by too many bees, and many, many, many more. But I know that I will never ever die in a fire because people like you, great people, would go into the fire to save an ordinary person like me. And that's what makes you so great, courageous, brave, terrific and wonderful special people.

Yours truly,

Claudia

We are laughing and crying at once imagining what the responders, tossing and turning in their sleep below, will feel when they open their eyes at dawn and see this.

Now that the vertical surfaces have been put to creative use, we tackle the challenge of organizing mountains of randomly stacked boxes. The ground floor is needed for services to the workers, so the upstairs is designated for supplies and storage. Because space is at a premium we must figure out ways to consolidate.

Up come the boxes from the first floor to the second: bottled water, Red Bull, clothes, medicine, toiletries, candy, power bars, pillows, blankets, sheets, towels, teddy bears—you name it. The pews upstairs are transformed into shopping aisles. We label the ends with alphabetical lists of contents. Order emerges from chaos. Supplies are made easily accessible. Our in-house commissary is created. We have more than we ever dreamed.

The ground floor is now relatively clear. More volunteers are carving out quadrants of services in the wide aisles that run the perimeter of the chapel's first floor. One section is designated for more cots where additional workers can sleep. People are making up beds. Another section is designated for chiropractors and massage therapists. Massage tables are moving into place. George Washington's large box pew is set up as the podiatrists' clinic. Gauze and implements are unpacked. An Israeli Hindu volunteer names these "the stations of compassion."

Just as we are contemplating the burned and blistered feet of the workers and the cure of their soles, our work is interrupted. The word is out on the street. Fred Luther has arrived.

Fred pulls up at the side gate of St. Paul's on Fulton Street at 1:00 a.m. Some police help unload the boots and organize the sizes. Others troop down to the site to let workers know the boots have arrived. As soon as the word goes out, little by little you can hear the roar of the machinery stop. Suddenly it's so quiet you can almost hear a pin drop.

Then out of the piles of gray dust, up over the mountains of debris, under the white glare of the stadium floodlights that illuminate the pile at night, hundreds of workers begin to stream out of the site and up

Fulton Street. One by one they walk up to Fred, receive their boots, remove their hard hats, and salute that trucker from North Carolina.

At the end Fred tells the guys he has a letter from a little seven-year-old girl back home. She wants Fred to give it to a firefighter and he asks if one of them would be willing to pose for a picture with it for her.

"No, no, no—not here," they say. "Come on with us."

Then they march Fred down to the pile and way up onto one of the hills of debris. Surrounded by hundreds of firefighters, holding the letter up, they take the picture with Fred's little disposable Kodak camera.

Fred and his buddy return to Seaman's and sleep a few hours, then get up early to help make deliveries all around the site. They do this until it is time to make the long trek home.

As they drive away a colleague remarks, "That fellow had a night he'll never forget." For that matter so did we all. A few weeks later Fred is back—this time with a thousand boots.

The sun rises on Sunday morning on a brand new church born in a very old space. The bones of the operation are in place. The food service is functioning on the front portico. Volunteers are spooning out ample portions cafeteria style from chafing dishes out there.

With some prodding we've convinced these nice Roman Catholic boys (as the vast majority are) to disregard their mother's voice chastising them in their heads. It's really okay to break the rules. Bring your food in the church.

The profusion of multi-colored banners and homemade cards from kids makes the place sparkle. This presence of so many people smiling down on us is like the communion of saints.

Beaming volunteers, honored to their depth to be standing in this place serving the men and women of Ground Zero, are manning tables everywhere. First is a table of all sorts of small personal items: lotion, lip balm, eye drops, throat lozenges, aspirin, cold medicine, nose spray. And next to that, a little deeper into the church, are the tables of clothing: sweatshirts, t-shirts, respirators, boots, socks, gloves, and so on. To your right is a piece of ecclesiastical furniture covered in reading material. On it is an array of magazines, newspapers, and some carefully vetted, inspirational pamphlets.

Then you arrive at the grand piano. The musicians' union of New York has organized a twenty-four hour rotation and their offerings are incredible. When they play you can feel the tremendous heart they are pouring into their gift.

When you reach the rear of the chapel the health-care stations begin. Massage tables run the entire length of the west side of the church. Workers are being massaged by the dozens. You don't usually find massage in the sanctuary of a church, but in this context it seems both beautiful and natural. Next are the chiropractors. One eighty-year-old practitioner has organized them all.

By now you have reached Washington's pew and the podiatrists. The remainder of the north aisle is filled with cots. The cots, and most of the pews in the center of the church, are adorned with blankets, pillows, and teddy bears. One worker is sleeping with two bears—one under each arm.

On the final side of the chapel, the east side, are the altar and the pulpit. Nuns and monks from communities up and down the East Coast are here keeping vigil in front of hundreds of twinkling votives. Lyndon and the bishop of the armed forces have scheduled a constant rotation of clergy. They are all now priests of the pile, trooping in and out in respirators and hard hats, serving at Lyndon's side. Together they are also conducting the daily Eucharist.

These are wonderfully chaotic services. A thousand or so workers, with their walkie-talkies squawking, are popping the tops on their soda cans, unwrapping the cellophane on their sandwiches. As the priest begins, "The Lord be with you," folks are being massaged. As we respond, "And also with you," foot washings are taking place. An ironworker gives the sermon while a bishop scrubs the floor.

These are early days, but the initial challenge has been met: to open our selves (and this building) to each other in a spirit of equality and mutual regard. We have consecrated our work to the valuing of human life, mindful of how much every person matters. As the firefighters saluted the trucker, we all salute each other for the courage to come and to care. And we pray that the chapel, spared from devastation, and standing strong amid the wreckage of violence and hatred, will continue to be a place where all people can better learn how to live together in harmony and joy, that our nation may be strengthened by the power that never dies. We have received the surprising gift of "that little bit inside" borne by thousands of people of every walk of life. We have received from each other the contagious passion of "whatever-it-takes." And now we embark together on the creation of a new kind of fellowship, as we serve one another in the little chapel that stood.

# CHAPTER 3

# LIFE TOGETHER

———◆———

THE RECTOR OF TRINITY ENTERS THE CHAPEL AND SURVEYS THE SCENE: the recent $100,000 paint job defaced by thousands of pieces of tape and tacks hammered into the walls; the deep gouges on all the pews left by the workers' gun belts; the hundreds of loaded guns lying in their discarded holsters on the floor while their owners sleep; the thousands of votive candles sputtering under the cards and letters, and, of course, the thousand or so people he has never seen before eating, talking, getting body rubs, and playing Trinity's grand piano. My stomach instantly twists in knots when I see the shock on his face. His gasp may be one of wonder but it is definitely not one of delight. With alarm in his voice he blurts out, "Who are all these weird people?"

He thanks me later, in his Christmas card, for my response: "Dr. Matthews, you must understand. All of this, every person, came to us. Everything came to us." I didn't know what else to say. Sometimes people do wonderful things we don't expect.

What has happened is definitely beyond the church's expectations. I can see how those used to control could have some trouble with this. After all, St. Paul's was just a museum. Only eight worshippers officially were on the church's rolls. And although Trinity had started to grow an "alternative congregation" at St. Paul's just before the attack, nobody could have anticipated just how radically "alternative" that flock would turn out to be.

The original concept for the new St. Paul's was yuppies: thousands at work among the sixty thousand employed within the towers. This was the "new demographic," lots of young professionals moving downtown and leasing a new crop of lofts. So the shift from Brooks Brothers to high-melting, bulletproof Kevlar body armor by itself is quite a surprise.

Unsurprisingly, I am soon called into our new temporary office for a chat with my boss. Jamie Callaway, God bless him, is supportive. He quietly gives me the room to put my old job in Grants on simmer and spend most of my time at St. Paul's. Jamie is a wise and patient man, and it seems I can see in his eyes an almost fatherly recognition that God is doing something in me that I cannot see at the time. He will not interfere, and I am extremely grateful for that. Without his support there is no way I could continue.

Dr. Matthews teases me about my transformed appearance. "Courtney, you look like a kid." I've arrived in jeans and my new red Doc Martin boots. On my shoulder is slung a backpack, my respirator is dangling, my cell with two-way is glued to my hand, and loads of official tags hang down my front where my pearls used to be. I can't quite read the way Matthews is looking at me. He appears to be puzzled by the overnight makeover and wondering, "What does it mean?"

The rector's two close advisors, Stuart and Linda, also want to talk. They are cautiously supportive and take me into their confidence. Some view what has happened at St. Paul's as risky. It cannot be denied that it is somewhat of a maverick operation. The challenge, as those who are not yet directly involved view it, is to bring the ministry into institutional structures and oversight to allay management's fears. That is not, however, what this spontaneous movement of people is about.

Which is not to say we aren't trying to establish some routines. The main staff gathers each morning in a small room at the rear of the chapel called the sacristy. This is the room where vestments, wine and wafers, altar linens, chalices, and candles are stored. It has also become our tiny office. It's a mess. We sit on upturned plastic buckets. An amplifier left from the pre-9/11 era of experimental liturgies has become our conference table in the middle of the room. There's a fax machine and a landline in the corner. Our laptops are stuck on window ledges. It's here that we huddle to figure things out as best we can.

Bethany must leave to return to North Carolina, but Katherine has decided to stay and carry on. On the outside Katherine is the quintessential southern belle, but inside she is a steel magnolia. Already, she's shown she won't give in to fear—not when daring to care is the gauntlet. With her gorgeous peaches and cream complexion, long curly red locks, and warm open heart, Katherine has been named the "sweetheart of Ground Zero." It would take a lot to undermine her commitment. Diane Reiners, an outstanding volunteer, also comes on staff to work side by side with Katherine.

Martin remains in charge of the food operation. Lyndon functions as chief pastor, spending a good deal of time in the pile. Sister Grace, a new addition from the Order of St. Margaret, steps into my old role as *ad hoc* chief of staff. The workers have fallen in love with her too. The police have brought her sergeant's stripes, pinned them on the sleeves of her habit, and given her the honorific, "Sergeant Grace." Fred and I take overnight shifts as supervisors and work to solidify support for the continuation of the ministry, running interference behind the scenes.

Lyndon, Katherine, Martin, Diane, and Grace establish the tone of the work. They are the ones who create the ways to implement and constantly reinforce the basic principles we all feel are essential for this to thrive. Theirs is the most important role, on the front lines. The demands on their capacity to be open and giving to everyone—with five thousand volunteers and ten thousand recovery and emergency personnel beginning to flow through—verge on the superhuman.

Thanks to Mary Morris, stationed at General Seminary, two shifts of twenty volunteers arrive each day, one at 6:00 a.m. and one at 6:00 p.m. In addition Martin creates a constant cadre of food captains and volunteers to deal with the logistics of serving thousands of donated meals. Lyndon and Grace also have their own rotation of clergy volunteers. It's becoming a big team of regular helpers.

We assume that the majority of volunteers arrive charged up and ready to go to work. It is notable that most have been inspired to come by the example of the first responders. At the beginning this is virtually all we have in common, but it is enough to make everything else possible. We don't take for granted the inspiration factor—the impact on people of the dramatic, altruistic example celebrated via the airwaves and every form of media far and wide. It's blitzing our brains in a very positive way—the constant repetition of emergency service personnel's choice to serve ordinary people at enormous cost to themselves. Service, sacrifice, and empathy are marks of the kind of leadership our country is lifting up. These values multiply our inspiration to be selfless contributors to a common goal.

In each story, I hear that the impassioned yearning to come was sparked in volunteers almost immediately. We're all from so many countries, backgrounds, and professions. But everyone who is here believed they could make a difference.

Barbara Horn, a graduate student from Milwaukee, explains to me how she came to help Martin with the food.

"When 9/11 happened I was watching it in Milwaukee. The tower came down, the smoke cloud went up, and I stood. It was like something happened in me. I didn't know what I was reaching for, I just had to come. I called a friend and asked, 'What can I do?' and she said, 'Just don't forget us.' So I said, 'I'll go and hold a sign at the Yankee Stadium service that says, 'Milwaukee Cares.' I thought, 'I can do that.' I knew there were tons of volunteers. I tried the Red Cross but they said you had to have Red Cross training. But I could still go and hold the sign.

"Then I got a call from a guy who said, 'What about St. Paul's Chapel?' So he gave me Martin's number and that's how I got in touch and connected with him."

For a musician from Finland name Ulla Suokko, recently graduated from Julliard, it happened this way: "I sat down and I looked up and I talked. As I say, I talked to the Universe. And you can even say I talk to God. But I say, 'Well, I'm here. Use me. Find a job that I can do.' You know I was by myself, but I have seen so many times when we say things out loud our words and visions and wishes have so much more power. So I said, 'I would really love to play at St. Paul's. How do I do that? Would it be possible?' And it was the next day that Ralph Ferris called and said, 'Ulla, my darling, we are organizing ourselves to play at St. Paul's Chapel. Would you like to join us?' And I said, 'Yes! I would love to do that.'"

And for Nehemiah Bar-Yahuda, a Hindu practitioner of healing touch from Israel, it happened this way: "I was in deep meditation and I was getting a very strong energy. The phone rang and it was a friend of mine, a woman I usually take care of. And she said, 'They bombed the World Trade Center.' Usually I would stop my practice but something told me to go deeper into meditation.

"The phone kept ringing and every time I knew I could not do anything about it. One call was from a yoga center that told me,

'Everybody is chanting to support the world.' I know something worse has happened. Still only after my hour meditation did I clear my space and call my friend and say, 'What happened?' She said, 'The World Trade Center collapsed."

"So the next thing that came to mind was, 'I have something I can offer.' I was born in crisis. I was born in Jerusalem in 1949 during the Yom Kippur war. My father was killed when I was three months. So this led me to study the healing process. I realize I can offer this back to people who live it now because this was not the first crisis in my life. So I knew what I was supposed to do and began to search my apartment for my massage certificate."

Fred is the one who raises the point that you may arrive wanting to give your all, but still be concerned about your capacity to do so. There are degrees of liberation from self-concern.

"If you are self-conscious or worried about your performance, about yourself, which I was when I first came," says Fred, "as I think every volunteer may be, there is a hurdle you have to get past. For me it was the experience of love in the environment that gave me the courage to open. People need that transformative moment.

"This place is becoming thick with the power of real collective love, and we want that to grow thicker. When the environment is thick with that power, when you know that and feel that, it totally changes everything."

We establish a way for volunteers to join the team that does what we call "beautification." That is to look around and think of ways to make the environment telegraph visually, even more powerfully than when you arrived, an ethos of collective caring, giving, and gratitude. The message is that thousands of individuals from diverse backgrounds, of myriad gifts, but the same feeling, are coming together here—and you are part of that.

Belief that caring is an active agent on the move, stirring the hearts of Americans to serve, is a fresh way of framing what faith is and does. It's so invigorating to see a church become a portal for this widespread movement, to see the church identified as a place people can plug in and make a difference for hurting people on the ground. People are obviously searching for that, and communities need to do this.

We want to reinforce that each contributor is welcomed as special and unique, but most powerful as a contributor when his or her gift is networked with all those gifts given by others. We know what seeing all the "stations of compassion" in action, and all the letters, cards, and banners, has done to us—how constantly seeing all of this keeps our hearts open and receptive to the continuous work of greater opening to more people. And we expect that the sight of all this will have a similar impact on others too.

Krystyna says, "I'm a photographer and I thought, 'It's really not my thing,' and I really didn't feel qualified, but the spirit and the joy and the love and the fellowship and the togetherness and the excitement and just being a part of the grace working there. The whole atmosphere is thick—you can cut the Holy Spirit with a knife. You know it is just so exciting and loving and the togetherness is just phenomenal. I think the big family is just irresistible. I don't have time, and sometimes I want to say, 'Forget it.' But still I keep coming back because of that."

Mary Morris says, "I walked in and thought, 'Wow! The blessings are everywhere.' It's the mixture of the experience of the visual, the sensory, the feeling, the touch, the smell. It is the connection between people. The whole ambience gives a tone of what is happening and makes us feel like it feels.

"The banners, the letters, the candles, the flowers, the supplies that somebody sent and somebody else stored. Seeing people eating and sleeping and resting and praying. And the beautiful music and prayers I feel not only being prayed in here but being prayed all over the world and encompassing us. It's the praying presence of thousands or even maybe hundreds of thousands."

Barbara Horn says, "The very first minute I walked in the door I got 'Bam! Wham!' Okay, I thought. Okay, I'll go with it. It was what was happening and you got immersed in it. It's like saying when you are baptizing someone full immersion, saying, 'When you were baptized did you feel the water?' I mean, where the heck were you? There was no choice. It wasn't like you said, 'Well, maybe I'll open myself up a little spiritually today.' No! You were overtaken unless you were completely into yourself. It was like I got on a rollercoaster and they started the thing and it's going. It scared the beejeezus out of me. It was the big shift. The seismic, spiritual earthquake. You walk in and somehow you get the vibe and it pushes you through."

We are all excited to begin to hear in detail the confirmation that the sight and feel of this huge collective opening and outpouring is so attractive and disarming to people. The power of scale is striking as people note "the big family," the phenomenal "togetherness," and the "presence of hundreds of thousands." The number of people represented makes it hard to avoid recognizing that this is about all of us—the nation, the human race.

Giving and serving is a way to discover the great joy of belonging within a thrilling whole. It makes me think of the Great Seal, the relationship between the glory of participating in a noble purpose, unity and true strength. It seems like we're recovering something both nations and churches are meant to be. Not competing tribes that draw lines between us. But collectives that gather us and give us contexts for living open lives of participation in something greater. As Barbara exclaimed to me one day, "Now this—this is life!"

Next we need to think about liberty. How do we frame a volunteer experience that in no way squelches this powerful impulse? Katherine and Diane are masters at determining how to do this. They are the ones who craft the briefing, the first interaction with volunteers after they walk in the door.

I watch Katherine gather the volunteers together in pews at the front of the church. She welcomes them to St. Paul's with her beaming countenance. She thanks them profusely for coming, and tells them, "For the next twelve hours this chapel is yours." She makes it explicit that they are free to contribute in any way that will add to the environment of care and concern for the workers.

There are only two rules at St. Paul's: no photographs and no trips into the site. To protect the workers' privacy, the former is reserved for the one photographer we've assigned that job to—Krystyna. The latter is reserved for pastors and chaplains working with Lyndon and the bishop of the armed forces. They are trained to deal with the disturbing, war-like conditions in the pile.

Other than that, volunteers are encouraged to be creative and to dream and implement new ideas to add to the community's life. People may be invited to consider a particular role but no one is assigned a duty. Everyone chooses, because we know that only an individual knows in his or her heart what they are burning to give. The level of commitment and enthusiasm poured into the task is so much greater when people are allowed to do what they do best and care about the most. That's the kind of energy we want to fill the air.

Then Katherine and Diane point out the various types of ministry taking place in the chapel. Volunteers can either support one of the existing efforts by joining an existing team, or if they look around and think of a new idea they want to implement, they can recruit a new team and resources to make it happen, post appeals on the Internet, do their own fundraising—be as creative, motivated, and effective as they feel moved to be. It is made explicit that we do this because we expect surprising gifts we could never imagine, from everyone who is here, and we welcome them.

To check on how this is working, I chat with a few volunteers. Generally they are stunned by our approach. None have ever worked in a volunteer capacity, especially in a church, where they are given so much room to direct their care toward solutions in any way they want.

One says, "I am amazed by our intuitive knowledge—this person should be left alone, this person should be touched, this person should be asked a question. We all just seem to know exactly what to do." People feel they have been liberated to find their basic nature, and when they discover it they also discover an innate knowledge of how to care for others.

Another says, "It feels like the perfect example of leadership in love because I feel like the people in charge really are not on a power trip. They are not imposing their ego. They are trusting different parts of the work to people they don't even know. We just show up at the door and we get to choose our task, given full trust. The staff is not looking after us or doubting, 'Can they do it?'

"A staff person said to me, "Would you like to take care of this?' I said, 'Okay.' And I did the best I could. I see that responsibility is shared in a very equal way. I haven't seen that anywhere. I wish we could create this in normal circumstances. It would be a perfect society if everybody was treated equal like this."

Martin says that he believes Lyndon plays a key role, as chief pastor. "So many people are down here in a volunteer capacity. Lyndon is particularly gifted in his ability to keep us working as a unit by allowing everybody to do what they do best—always saying, 'Yes,' You get a lot of yes answers from him. If I ask him, 'Should we do this?' the answer is, 'Yes.' 'This?' 'Yes.' His attitude is making St. Paul's successful."

It is not an exaggeration to say that the result of so much liberty and affirmation to be compassionate is nothing less than euphoric. The mood that is gathering, as we are freed to make a difference, neither holding ourselves back or being restrained by others, is one of extraordinary excitement. One of the greatest difficulties is persuading volunteers they must leave at the end of their shift. Even after twelve hours people don't want to go.

Barbara tries to describe it. "I'm a doubter. I can go along with the fact that Jesus existed. Dr. King existed and Gandhi existed, so people of great fortitude and love have existed. I'd like to have that kind of faith. It's my role model. And here you see this whole big thing and go "Oooooh! I would really like that." It's like lollipops of faith. It's like Candyland. It's like, Wow! Headquarters. The Vatican of Spirituality. It is there. It is happening. It is wonderful—so alive. It is like a magnet, and I want more and more, so I get can to the bigger faith. I just never want to leave and I think that is true for everybody."

The pace at which new ideas are added changes the appearance and feel of the chapel daily. The space feels like it is alive, which makes it an exhilarating place to be. Particularly since all the ideas are born of incredible thoughtfulness toward others. Lyndon talks about how we are playing a wonderful sacred game: "outdoing one another in acts of kindness."

One volunteer suggests wake-up calls so workers don't have to worry about sleeping through their next shift. Another suggests a thank-you letter program that involves the workers and volunteers in answering the letters from children. Another team from South Carolina introduces New Yorkers to a delicious cheese grits recipe for breakfast. One creative person sees a blanket covered in the hundreds of patches left by search and rescue teams who've come from around the country to serve in the site. She suggests we pin them all on Lyndon's red chasuble, the robe clergy wear to celebrate the Eucharist each day. It makes for the most moving vestment I have ever seen a priest wear.

Another decides his calling is to sit quietly and anonymously at the foot of each worker's cot. As he or she is sleeping the volunteer prays for them like his grandmother used to do in the night for him when he was a boy. An idea that turns our gates that encircle the churchyard into the major shrine at Ground Zero also comes from a volunteer. She suggests buying large sheets of blank canvas, hanging them on the fences around the churchyard, and posting volunteers with markers so visitors can sign them with a prayer or message to the workers and families. This inspires our artist in residence, Jess Stamen, an art student from the Cooper Union, to organize a team of artists to make extraordinary banners, emblazoned with words like "Courage" and

"Hope" for the exterior of the chapel. The next thing we know, thousands of visitors outside the chapel are leaving their unique imprint. The perimeter soon looks like Westminster Abby in the days following the death of Princess Diana. It is remarkable.

All of this is captured and posted on the Internet, and the number of participants and donors rises exponentially. Just as Fred envisioned, with each passing day the presence of the power of real love grows even thicker. We continue to be astounded by what comes out when people are inspired and free: the infinite multiplication of outward visual representations of the inward beauty human beings carry. In our eyes the chapel is becoming a deeply sacramental space, but in a very populist, democratic idiom.

But the chapel is not only about joy and elation. It is also filled with grief, and people suffering from terrible wounds. Douglas Brown who was with us the day of the attack has been serving as a chaplain in the pile, and he describes it this way.

"The chapel is crackling with energy, and the energy is all around caring for others. There is great solemnity about it too. It's dense and more complex than I thought it would be. There is such a sense of awe of what we're all engaged in. We can never forget why we are here. So there is an awesomeness about it, and also an extraordinary feeling of mutual availability—of perfect strangers opening their hearts to each other."

A crazy thing—it is pain but it is joy.

At the front gate a woman is agitated. She is desperate to come in. Martin intervenes and asks, "What's wrong?"

She is writing something. Writing on a picture, "Thank you for finding our Brad." The morgue has just identified the remains of her son—twenty-two years old. So handsome.

Martin says, "Would you like to come in?"

She replies, "I think I need to."

The woman, her dog, and a small entourage of relatives strike out across the chapel for a cluster of workers and volunteers. They are sharing the photo with them. "This is our Brad. Thank you. Thank you for finding our Brad."

Everyone is in tears. They are hugging and thanking everyone. There are more deep hugs and more tears. It is a fervent exchange.

Later Martin explains, "I just completely lost it. It was the pain in her face. I've never felt the pain someone else is feeling like I did right then.

It really went deep—how much hurt from the loss of someone you love. I got the human condition. My soul was taken to a place I was not consciously aware of before. I was feeling the hurt and the pain and sadness and love and joy in there right next to the pain and the hurt. It wasn't morbid. It was just connected. Really, really connected."

As beautifully as the ministry is blossoming, there is also tension. Two philosophies are beginning to conflict. The vicar, who has oversight of both the mother church and St. Paul's, is deeply concerned to wrestle order out of the chaos of our radical little cocoon. He has spent very little time in the chapel, leaving that to Lyndon as priest-in-charge. He is not having the firsthand experiences we are.

My sense is that he is skeptical and believes an operation like ours will soon implode. He wants to see an organizational chart with names for our various positions and reporting lines—no small feat given the organic way in which this operation has grown and developed. One night I work until the wee hours drawing and redrawing the chart until I know it will convince him we have a comprehensible system. Alerted by the anthrax scare, we have also put our heads together to develop an operations manual that deals with procedures in case of emergency and other prudent systems. All of this is wise and reasonable, and we happily comply. But the spirit of the requests has felt negative.

Now we are meeting to discuss Thanksgiving. The vicar wants to open St. Paul's to the public and Trinity's congregation (still without access to their church building) for a Thanksgiving service. Katherine disagrees. She explains the workers have come to depend on the safety of the chapel's environment as a place they can unlock their grief away from prying eyes. For pastoral reasons Katherine thinks it's insensitive. In the end, however, we acquiesce.

Still we want to do an especially delicious Thanksgiving dinner, as the teams in the pile will not have the holiday off. So many have been separated from families for nearly two months. Wouldn't it be nice, we suggest, to invite spouses and children to join us for the Thanksgiving meal?

The vicar forbids it. Up till now I have believed that his concerns have to do with safety and the protection of property. Now I am not so sure. The vicar says something revealing. "These workers are being paid on the American taxpayer's dime. They should eat their dinner quickly, and then get back in the pile. If their spouses come they'll take longer over their food. I don't want family members invited." I instantly think of the hurt it would cause if this were said to the workers' faces. The vicar does not understand the betrayal of his comment because he has not drawn close. I wonder if I would have shared his perspectives only a few weeks earlier.

The next day I have a conversation with Joe Bradley that I will never forget. Joe is a legend. He was the first crane operator to arrive at Ground Zero and is now one of the foremen clearing the north quadrant of the pile. Joe begins at the beginning, when he arrived at Ground Zero on September 12 as part of the first search and rescue team. He is very open with me about what is happening in his inner life.

"As I walked toward the site," Joe says, " I walked down Church Street and prayed for the courage to stay together because at twenty-two I'd helped build the World Trade Center. My thoughts were racing and I was kind of mixed up. But the Twenty-third Psalm came into my head. The dust and the ashes and debris—all I could hear was, 'As I walk through the valley of the shadow of death I fear no evil.'

"I finally reached the shadow of One Liberty Plaza. I had just spotted a buddy when they sounded the emergency whistle. Suddenly fifty firefighters were running toward me and I didn't know what was going on, I just ran with them. People falling. People picking people up. We ran to the Battery Park Tunnel. Then I walked up West Street and saw my crane and the guy who dispatched me out. No orders. No money. No services. Nothing. Just volunteers trying to help.

"I ran into a fire chief who said he'd like to clear a debris field with heavy iron on top. I turned around. There were four or five ironworkers there. They asked if I had a crane and I said yes. So they said they'd like to work with me. So I had a machine and a crew. Like a miracle twenty-five firefighters showed up right then with tanks and torches. Then we had a mission so we went to work. No supervision. No foreman. We worked as smooth as you can imagine. Everything went perfectly, but we were soaking wet, working in eighteen inches of water straight through the night. And all night long they blew the whistle thinking Liberty Plaza was coming down. That happened four or five times that night and I thought to myself, 'Joe, you came here to die.'

"I prayed for darkness because I couldn't handle what I was seeing. The first body was a lady in a business suit. Middle aged. It was remarkable. She wasn't even dirty. We laid her down on the stretcher and fixed her eyes and her lapels. I remember the firefighter on the back of the stretcher fell, but he lifted his arms up over his head as he went down so the body wouldn't hit the ground.

"After that I was sitting on the curb with my head in my hands. It was the middle of the night. That's when the Salvation Army kids appeared in their sneakers with their pink hair and their bellybuttons showing and bandannas tied around their faces. One was a little girl pushing a shopping cart full of eyewash through the muck. They came with water and cold towels and took my boots off and put dry socks on my feet. And we kept going all night on the twelfth and the morning of the thirteenth and were relieved in the afternoon.

"I've never seen so many people pull together. One unit. One thought. We were going to rescue a survivor. But that wasn't to be.

"When I was finally relieved and started to walk out, I thought to myself, 'You did pretty good. You did your part. You can go home and get back to normal. Then my mind flashed to the hostages coming home from Iran, and the ticker tape parade when the Yankees won the World Series. I had always thought that's what New York's about—those kinds of heroes. But it was the little girl with the pink hair who became my hero that night. Not Tino Martinez.

"And then when I got to Houston Street a bunch more of these kids, all pierced and tattooed with multi-colored hair had made a little make-shift stage. And they started to cheer as we came out. That was it for me. I never identified with those people before, but I started crying and I cried for four blocks. I can't . . . tell you. I was taken so off guard by their behavior.

"I've been a construction worker my whole life and I've always felt I was viewed by the public as a pest. As crude. And now I was so vulnerable. Yep. I was taken totally off guard.

"I got home to my wife, who asked, 'Joe, are you okay?' 'Sure!' I said. You know, the bravado came right back. But she said, 'Are you sure? Go look in the mirror.' There I was with my filthy dirty face, and just two clean lines down from my eyes.

"You become like a child when you get banged around a bit. She cried with me. Gave me something to eat. Drew a bath . . . I don't take baths. She put me to bed for six or seven hours. I told her I wasn't coming back. But here I am. I haven't missed a day.

"It was almost like a tunnel the way everybody came together. The first week I had my two-hundred-and-fifty-ton triple A to begin with. The next week my thousand-ton triple A crane arrived. It was amazing to see firemen and police hugging each other. Unions who refused to work together buried the hatchet. There was search and rescue from every state.

I've learned a lot about good and evil. I've learned a lot about the power of prayer. I never knew anything about Episcopalians, or Presbyterians, or gays, or people with nuts and bolts through their cheeks, or those Broadway people, but now I know them all. We're not the heroes. They are the heroes. They've cried and prayed out loud for me. I never thought I'd have a family like this one."

———————

After talking to Joe I have to take a walk. I am overwhelmed by the beauty and pain of his testimony. I had no idea. It's complex and profoundly moving. I have to walk and breathe. Especially when I think of what the vicar said.

The cost and the tragedy of not valuing equally all who live in our society registers deep inside me. Before this I've never had an intimate, one-on-one conversation with someone who has experienced the pain of being labeled by people as less than. In the same breath Joe confesses the feeling of being released from viewing others that way. Compassion is what performs the double healing. Together we've created that kind of fellowship—that kind of human family. This is what the church has come to stand for and we must remain true to the trust that has been placed in us for being that.

We are learning to feel what it is like to walk in another's boots. Not only because we are having the kinds of verbal exchanges Joe and I just had. In many cases we're also either accepting help from or offering assistance to folks we previously thought had nothing to give.

In the course of this day that begins with the conversation with Joe, my allegiance is pledged specifically to this feature of what the church can be. If we can continue to do this, exchanging help in spite of age-old accretions of pointless defensiveness and groundless disapproval, this work has the promise to change completely where we stand in relation to one another. We have believed we could make a difference. Now we have a bigger opportunity than I ever dreamed. This is a tremendous eye-opener for me. I've never thought of service as a potential instrument of justice until I heard Joe describe his moment with the pink-haired girl. Love really and truly overcomes.

After some serious pacing, and talking out loud to myself, I return to sit with Jimmy Abbanando and Jerry Krusch, partners in the NYPD force. On the day of the attack Jimmy and Jerry were assigned to search rooftops for casualties. Since then they have been at Ground Zero every day. My mind is again blown, this time by the sweetness of the first New York cops I've ever had a heart-to-heart with. This is how they describe their new routine and the inner feelings this new experience is stirring in them.

Jimmy starts, "Well first of all when we come to the chapel in the morning they pray for us. It's like we're a family. The chapel is our second home and to tell you the truth the beds are more comfortable than mine at home.

"Then there's the thought that so many of the volunteers have come from out of state. Like the eleven-year-old girl from Chicago I met this morning. For her birthday present she asked to come here and help."

Jerry continues, "It's so touching. Like Katherine Avery. She comes from South Carolina and uproots her whole life."

Jimmy adds more. "Really there's an outpouring of love from around the world. The support of people coming to pay their respects really means a lot. So we thought about it and decided it's important to meet people and listen to them express their feelings. But nobody ever trained us to do this. You know in the police department they don't teach that."

I ask them to describe their day in greater detail.

Jerry starts, "Well, we cover the entire area. We listen to stories. You can look into the crowd and see who needs help. People cry on our shoulders. They also express how sorry they are for the NYPD's loss."

Jimmy gives some examples. "We see lots of family members coming for closure. If there are children we go out of our way to take them down to the site. We go to St. Paul's and get the medals from Sister Teresa's order or rosaries. I remember one little Spanish girl whose father died. We took her down to the site and said a prayer, then we took her to the church and gave her an angel pin and told her she would always have a guardian angel."

Jerry remembers another visitor. "The cousin of the pilot of the first plane came down the last day of November, and she didn't know if she could handle it. But we took her down and helped her through it. "

Jimmy summarizes, "This is what we do. But in our spare time we've written one hundred and thirty thank you letters. We get a photo of the Trade Center to send to those who have written a letter to the chapel. They took the time to write us. The least we can do is acknowledge their caring from so far away."

When I ask them how this experience has changed them, the theme of the human costliness of their chosen vocation and the thankless diminishment they receive in return that bothered me so much with Joe rears its ugly head again.

Jerry begins, "Most cops don't get to bond with people. Nobody calls us for happy occasions. This experience is good for us. The friendships we've made. The relationships. Did you know at Easter we are going to talk to a Sunday school class? This is more than, 'Hi. Hello.' We've seen how it's possible to touch people. It's the sense that you've touched people more than you'll ever know. We've never gotten to do this with people before."

Jimmy finishes, "People didn't like us. And they didn't like New Yorkers. We've got everybody here, no matter their ethnicity. People didn't like that. But now it's touched everybody, and people tell us all the time something no one ever said to us before, 'You guys are amazing.'"

I go for another walk. What is happening to us? Here are two cops behaving like they are priests. These are individuals who have been working fourteen-and-a-half-hour days, seven days a week, including their day off when they come down as unpaid volunteers. And yet they too let slip that they have spent a lifetime being inaccurately stereotyped by others as policemen and "ethnic" New Yorkers. Their vocation has been costly and isolating, excluding them from opportunities to relate to their fellow human beings in ways that have been painful to them. Parts of their humanity have been diminished in the past, but they are being healed and liberated too.

I return to the chapel to have yet another chat. This one is with two sanitation workers named Tony Palmeri and Joe Bacetty. I know them the best of all those I've spoken with today. But this time the conversation will go deeper. I brace myself to hear more along the same lines.

We begin by talking about the nature of their work at the site. Joe begins.

"We've done a lot of sludge cleaning, and hosing down sludge. Everybody has a job to do and that is part of ours."

Tony picks up, "We are doing that. We are doing everything—everything except recovering body parts. We also do the carting—millions of tons. For me I'm proud of who I am and my job. I'm an honest guy and I do what I gotta do.

"But sometimes I feel a bit strange when somebody asks me and I say I'm a sanitation worker. I always have in the back of my mind that they might be saying, 'But you're a garbage man.' I feel like I'm doing well. We are doing more than just cleanup. Everybody pitches in and we get the job done."

Joe slips a few words in. "But to be appreciated . . ." His voice trails off and there is silence.

Suddenly Tony's on fire. "We're down in the hole doin' the work . . ."

Joe interjects, "Our supervisors are pounding us . . ."

"Yeah," Tony says. "It's like hell. And then you see the volunteers wanting to help you. We get the love, the respect, the congratulations, the pats on the back, the thank you's from every person! I can't really believe people are so wonderful and caring. They don't care I'm a sanitation worker. They don't care I am heavy. They don't care I am Catholic. What they care about is me as a person. They care about me! They really want to help me! It's just wonderful. If not for a place like St. Paul's, you, Katherine, people all over who turn around and say thank you, we would feel like nothing."

Joe quietly interjects again, "So, so this is heaven. How do you make someone understand?"

Tony elaborates, "In the chapel we look at each other and we know we are feeling the same thing. Volunteers look in my eyes and say, 'Wow!' And I look in their eyes and say, 'Wow!' You kinda have a bond between ya and words don't have to be spoken. The love and the caring people are giving. Not because of who I am. Not because of what I do. We want to convey that little bit we have inside to each other.

"If you could just move people in that direction and make them understand how it is to blend together and not worry. Cause ya know, we're pretty good together. But unless we can make each other feel that way I don't think it's possible for there ever to be any real, real harmony in this world."

I'm done for the day. There is no way I could hear anymore in this twenty-four-hour period. I didn't think it was possible, but I feel closer, more admiring and protective of my new friends than ever before.

It keeps taking me back to my moment on the subway with the Sikh. How many people on this journey will I discover who are judged in our society by something other than their character? How many people are there in this country making incredible contributions to our common lives but feel like they are nothing? How do they stay beautiful without receiving the acknowledgement, appreciation, and regard we owe to them? Why do we do this to each other? Something is wrong and needs to change.

Over dinner with Katherine I discuss my impressions with her. She is also struck by what has captured me.

"Yes," Katherine says. "This work is about all of us and all of our differences. The divisions between us are beginning to disappear and you have to be okay with letting them go. We're not doing anything complicated. We're just serving coffee, food, handing out medicine. But you begin to understand these men and women have been shunned in different ways all their lives. It's so powerful because we're celebrating the lives of everyone.

"I'm with fireman Robert and he smells of decaying bodies. I don't have words for this. We hug him. We've created a space where people are free to do that. It's enormous to me to see us all that way. Sitting around in our socks. Talking about our day. You can't go in St. Paul's and stay separate. The barricades society wants to put between us mean nothing. Because we're helping each other and loving each other and that's it."

It feels incredibly important and precious—sacred. I know this is hope, what is happening between us. But I cannot bear to think that Americans of such decency, heart, and character are amazed to be treated well by other Americans. Their disbelief in being honored and celebrated—that place in their heart breaks mine. There is a kind of healing going on in this chapel that has nothing to do with the attack. We have inflicted these wounds on each other.

And yet I keep coming back to hope. It is incredible to me to think that all it really takes to dismantle divisions, heal wounds, and establish new ways of relating is, in Katherine's words, "helping each other and loving each other and that's it." Can we do that for each other? Are we willing to invest ourselves in that? Are we willing to give up something for that? The fellowship in the chapel is proving we are, we can, and we will.

It never would have occurred to me that in the course of the recovery from 9/11 we would come together in a way that would begin to reveal and heal some of our country's self-inflicted wounds beneath the surface of things. Uncovering this adds a new layer of importance to what is happening here. I have become very sensitive since the bombing to the slightest diminishment or hurt inflicted on other people, but the way I feel about the possibility of dishonoring or hurting our heroes given what they are enduring for us, and what it means to them to receive appreciation that is long overdue, is beyond the capacity of language to describe.

It upsets me so much I have to pray hard about it, and in the course of doing that I'm led to delve into a body of writings I have not visited for some time: the speeches and sermons of Dr. Martin Luther King Jr. It was King who wrote that justice is love working to correct all that opposes love. We began here believing that a huge amount of collective love and active reverence for human life existed and would combine and work to correct the damage done by the attack. Now I am seeing that same collective love beginning to correct the damage we've done to each other. Maybe this is a sign of new times.

A few weeks later, at the Harvard Mind-Body Medical Institute conference in Boston, I share with an audience of nearly a thousand people my conversations with Joe Bradley, Jimmy and Jerry, and some of Katherine's story. Lyndon somehow finds the time to produce an incredible short film about the workers set to the Five for Fighting hit, "It's Not Easy to Be Me."

Fred describes the extraordinary self-organizing miracle of the free, open, and evolving chapel. The self-organizing system that has materialized is stunning in its scope and effectiveness. The Internet has played an unprecedented role in linking us together with partners across the country and the world. He shows how the power of independent initiative networked via the church signals a new civic role for institutions like ours. St. Paul's has become a portal for a large and complex network of altruists. We've never thought of the church as a hub for such diverse self-organizing mobilization on this scale before.

The response from the audience is overwhelming. They stand and cheer—it seems like forever. It's the first time we've told our story to anyone, so we're a bit bowled over by the response. It is yet another confirmation in my eyes that we as a people in this country are wrestling with the same human issues dominating the chapel's life. The events of 9/11 have triggered this. And yet there are still those at home in New York who seem to be frightened, not encouraged by the overwhelming momentum that is attaching to the chapel—larger and larger numbers by the day.

When I return to New York, I decide it is important to check the volunteer perspective on some of the issues raised by the workers. One obvious place to start is with Mary Morris, since she has been recruiting a large proportion of the national church volunteers.

Mary says, "What I hear volunteers taking away from their experience, and I feel this myself, is 'we're all in this together and we're all the same.' I finally understand we're all the same. To think—sanitation workers, the firemen—I never knew firemen. They aren't a part of my culture—my ethnic culture. I didn't think it could happen. But my joy in life now is being blessed by them.

"And when you are equal there's endless possibilities of communion and community. When volunteers walk in that door they experience the same amount of love as the workers. It is unconditional and it is so overpowering. When you are in that chapel you know that every creature in the room is loved as much as you, and you are loved more than anybody. I mean there is no quantity to it. The shift I'm hearing is, 'We were so loved by everybody and everybody else is so loved by everybody, for the first time we are all equal.'

"Somehow our facades are stripped and our barriers. There's something about watching a construction worker sobbing. It kind of takes your breath away—the concept that a construction worker could actually be that moved. I mean, I never really thought about it. My preconceptions about a lot of things have been thrown out the window."

I'm sitting with Nehemiah Bar-Yahuda, who has been doing bodywork on firemen and all the workers. "It was not in my environment, working people, blue collar people. I did not think of them being so charitable. These are people of great charity and great spirituality. But the people I have known involved in charity are college people. And now we are working with people from all classes of life, and we are all aiding the same purpose—to serve people."

These kinds of remarks are honest and encouraging, and yet the subtext is clear. The negative stereotypes the two Joes, Jimmy, Jerry, and Tony have felt throughout their professional lives were not imaginary. They were real. Amazingly we have struck upon a way of living together that is correcting these and bringing the barriers down.

We're doing it in a community that reinforces the enormous collective capacity we have as members of the human race when we pool our individual gifts and passion to care and be concerned with others. The beauty of the totality of "that little bit we have inside" when combined collectively is so awe-inspiring, it is hard to gain an experiential taste of that and still wish to exclude any potential contributor. It also helps us feel loved and safe, and therefore less inclined to cruelty or condescension.

But if we stay in our silos, how do we ever give ourselves an opportunity to taste the beauty and power of this? I'm reminded of the way Katherine expressed herself on the topic: "The barricades society wants to put between us mean nothing." As long as forces can keep these internal or external "barricades" in place, we have no experience of what life is like without them. That is why we must see that we are free to say to ourselves and to the wider society, "to us they mean nothing," and create these new fellowships of the future.

I now see our initial choice to open the chapel gates, as the altruistic stampede gathered and stormed us, was full of grace. I am glad we did not ask permission. I'm realizing as we live into this that our original decision to let it all in, then to set the tone and expectation that everyone is an equally valued contributor, were far more countercultural decisions than any of us recognized at the time.

So was the choice to blare from every inch of wall space that any one contributor, though valued as unique and precious, is partial, not the whole. Then the great collective begins to be seen. And when it is seen it converts, working against the exclusion and diminishment of anyone. Love correcting all that opposes love.

It also seems that when all are expected, received, liberated to give and appreciated for doing so, as Mary puts it, "when everybody is so loved," the motives for creating barriers that exclude or stereotypes that diminish begin to melt away. I cannot imagine what we'll see if we keep moving in this direction, but I'm certain Lyndon is right: "Don't Stop Here."

## CHAPTER 4

# THE TORCH

———◆———

AS THE OLD YEAR WANES THE VICAR INSISTS ON KNOWING THE ANSWER
to a dogged question he poses to us regularly: "When is St. Paul's going
to be a church again?"

I am a theologian, and the answer to his question begs a definition
not a date. Lyndon has replied politely but firmly, "I don't think St.
Paul's has ever been more of a church." Thus the contours of the
debate are drawn. Most in our circle would agree with Lyndon. Part
of the difficulty in this dispute is that the church we are trying to steward is the church of the future not the church of the past.

New manifestations of old institutions and the change these represent do not happen without friction. There are always traditionalists
who see the new as a loss, and they are right, it is. I have been one of
those traditionalists. Years of my life have been spent studying the
church of the past, enthralled with the quaint beauty of bygone ages.
But just as 9/11 has become a watershed for me in so many other ways,
my rendezvous with violent death has also marked a turning point for
me on this issue. I no longer think humankind has the luxury of
indulging in dollhouse religion. The size of the problems we face has
made me an ardent champion of ecclesiastical innovation and the
church of the future.

It is the season of Advent, the time in the church calendar when we
mark with anticipation the coming of Christmas—the incarnation of

God with us—and the coming of God's kingdom. Hoards of silent pilgrims come to Ground Zero in droves. New deliveries of Christmas cards and homemade presents from children arrive by the thousands. *New York Magazine* reports that volunteering at St. Paul's is "one of the ten best things about Christmas in New York." *Time Out* says it's harder to get a volunteer slot at the chapel than a ticket to see the hit *The Producers* on Broadway. NY1, the twenty-four-hour news station in the city, names St. Paul's New Yorker of the Week. Garrison Keillor's weekly radio show, *A Prairie Home Companion*, begins its broadcast with the performance of a haunting, vaguely Irish lullaby, dedicated to the miracle chapel. It's entitled "A Thin Space," the Celtic term to describe a place on earth shot through with the presence of the divine. To me these are all proofs that this incarnation of church may not be conventional, but it certainly speaks to many as something valuable and true.

One of the features of this "Chaotic Hotel of Radical Hospitality" that is becoming more heightened by the day is the multi-faith character of our congregation. Our diversity is not simply across occupation, income, class, age, and ethnicity. It is also across religions. My mother and I have agreed to supervise the Christmas Eve overnight shift and have been met with a surprising present from a synagogue. Members of B'Nai Jeshurun, which has sent eight hundred volunteers to the chapel over the past several months, has now offered to fill all of the volunteer slots on Christmas Eve night so that Christian brothers and sisters may celebrate the holy day at home.

St. Paul's is everyone's, but the Jewish presence among us is particularly large and strong. It's almost as if L'Enfant, when he chose the *Shekinah* as the subject of St. Paul's altarpiece, somehow knew this day would come.

Barbara Horn has told me about two Jewish volunteers, Paula and Avi, who accosted her with their excitement one day. "Hey, guess what! Guess who did all the readings for the Eucharist today?" Barbara looked at them skeptically and said, "Not you? You did the first reading right?" "No!" they said. "We did all the readings." "You did what?" Barbara replied. "Yep. We did them all. The Jews. This is our church."

Ulla Suokko has also described several experiences she's had that have made a lasting impression. She is not particularly enthralled with institutional religion, but this is so different from anything she's ever seen before.

"There was an Emergency Medical Services memorial and one of the speakers was a rabbi from FDNY. The first thing he said was, 'It is an honor to walk in this beautiful little church that is so full of love and so full of sacredness.' And I was thinking, 'Wait a minute. This rabbi is talking in a Christian church.' It moved me so thoroughly because I realized that is the kind of spirit that we have come to share. It does not matter. We have come together.

"The rabbi continued. He said, 'The cross is one of the most beautiful symbols of humankind because it points straight to heaven and across to each other. Now is the time to strengthen that across to each other and come together as human beings.' And I thought, 'Alleluia! Amen!' I was really, really moved.

"I thought, 'Thank you God because this is what we need. We need to come together.'"

In the midst of Hanukkah, Lyndon shares a service with Rabbi Gelman and one hundred members of Congregation Kehilath Jeshurun. All report being deeply moved by a deep sense that the Spirit of God, so alive in this space, is profoundly present with everyone. Gelman tells the sacred story that is the basis for this holy season, when the Maccabees were driven from the Temple and the Hebrews relit the eternal flame. And although there was only enough oil for one day, the flame miraculously lasted for a week.

After retelling the story of the miracle of the eternal flame in Hebrew tradition, Gelman, a well-known media figure in New York and seldom at a loss for eloquent words, is suddenly choked with emotion. He pauses, and then makes a confession to the assembled that he has never liked Hanukkah because of its commercialization. "But here in a Christian church," he says, "I am experiencing Hanukkah for the first time." The Rabbi links the celebration of that miracle, hope coming out of devastation, light out of darkness, to the work that is transforming our despair.

Ulla is the one who tells me another story that sheds light on why this multi-faith unity is happening to us so naturally.

"There was a lady, a psychologist, who volunteers on Thursdays. She and I were talking in a pew. And I said to her, 'You know, I am not really a churchgoer-type person, but I think I have found my church.' And by that I meant the church we have created in our hearts by connecting with each other. And she said, 'You know, I have found my church too—and I am Jewish.' And I thought, 'That is so cool.'

"This is the thing. At St. Paul's we can be Jewish or Christian or nothing. Or we can be black or white or anything. I am from Finland, yet I feel this is a human effort, not only even an American effort. It was the World Trade Center. It was an attack on all of us. Here everyone is a part of the amazing grace. We are here as a human nation. We do not draw borders and say, 'This is mine.' We have to be in this together and we have to help each other see that."

One afternoon at twilight, when light flakes of snow are beginning to fall from the sky, three bearers of wisdom arrive at our gates: Karen Armstrong, Jim Wallis, and Elizabeth Kubler-Ross. The presence of all three, come to see this new infant incarnation of what it means to be the church, is yet another confirming sign for me.

Jim Wallis, an evangelical pastor who has been called "God's Democrat," is head of the Sojourners community headquartered in Washington, D.C., and author of numerous books on social justice, faith, and political life. The gift he gives to me is a statement I will never forget, as we finish our walk of the pile and the chapel. He turns, far away in pensive thought and says thoughtfully, reverently, "This is truly a place of pilgrimage. Do you know why?" I say, "No," intensely curious what Wallis's answer will be. "Because," Jim says, "it is a place that changes you simply by coming to it."

This is a great affirmation because Wallis, a passionate evangelical activist, is hardly one to respect indulgent forms of postmodern spirituality. His conversion text from the Bible, as he often says publicly, is Matthew 25: "As you have done it unto the least of these you have done it unto me." He believes that spirituality must be disciplined by a concern for justice or else he believes it becomes sadly narcissistic. "We buy the books, we buy the tapes. We hear the guru speaker. Barnes & Noble has a whole wall of how to be spiritual, balanced, healed, whole. Spirituality becomes a commodity to be bought and sold. So spirituality has to be disciplined by social justice."

I think everyone in our fellowship would agree. Compassion in action is teaching us more about faith as a real agent for change and healing in the world than a dozen self-help books ever could. I think we qualify as a social justice ministry. After all, in our case a group of citizens has moved into a place of deep suffering, commandeered a church, created a cell that turns many unjust social norms on their head, and declared such a radical reverence for life that we dig for the lost even in the land of the dead.

As Jim departs I turn my attention to the great Swiss scholar, Elizabeth Kubler-Ross, who pioneered a field with her seminal work, *On Death and Dying*. She is here despite her impairment from a stroke, deeply engrossed in examining the children's cards and letters from her wheelchair. A friend from San Francisco, Gary Malkin, who is here today too, has recorded Kubler-Ross for his moving series "Wisdom of the World," and is stunned to see her out and about. "I saw her last in the hospital after her stroke. I never would have imagined seeing her recuperated and strong enough to sustain an effort like this." We both realize this could be one of the last acts of Kubler-Ross's life.

The gift she brings for me is the reminder of where her incredible life's work as a scholar probing the mystery of death began. It was in Maidenek, in a concentration camp where she went as a young student just after the liberation in 1945. She wanted to see how children, who had lost their families, their homes, their schools, and everything, approached their deaths in the gas chambers. She found that the walls in the camp were filled with pictures of butterflies that all these children had drawn in the days before they died. It was incomprehensible to her. Thousands of children going into the gas chamber, and this the message they leave behind—a butterfly.

I've never been able to relate to this story before. But now I can see, I think, how the butterflies represent surrender to the apprehension of something in the face of death. I hope fervently I am learning to see and embrace this beauty, that I will apprehend before I die—what I believe the children who drew the butterflies saw: the sacred Beauty intoned in the life that surrounds and outlasts us, and whose apprehension puts preoccupation with the mortal individual self in its proper perspective.

If one can come to experience this Beauty as greater and more riveting than the individual "I" even in the face of inevitable death, then one is freed. Free from ego, selfishness—everything that constricts, chains, and mars our perception of the world around us, and prevents discovery of joy, of life. In the Buddhist tradition it is called enlightenment. In the Christian tradition the same insight is captured in the familiar phrase, "He who would save his life must lose it." Seeing Kubler-Ross reminds me of the black cloud, and how it was the beginning of my release.

And then there is Armstrong, walking the aisles of the chapel with Fred. I want to pinch myself to make sure this is all really happening—so many spiritual greats, here all at once. There is so much in her corpus of thought that would draw her to want to see this place. Foremost, I think, would be her concern with human violence, as something perpetrated by both religious and secular people.

Armstrong argues that we cannot pin this terrible trait of violence on either religion or secularism. She reminds her audiences constantly that this is a human trait, part of the human reality. In an interview with Bill Moyers she elaborates, "Atrocity is what human beings do. Secularism can be just as murderous, just as lethal as religion. One of the reasons religion developed in the way that it did over the centuries was precisely to curb this murderous bent that we have as human beings."

I think this is a starting place for arguing how our new church, our church of the future, is in continuity with the ancient tradition. Post-9/11, in a new millennium begun with this dramatic, murderous act, perhaps we are responding out of this ancient knowledge, refocusing mission on what our world most urgently needs right now. "To curb the murderous bent that we have as human beings."

In the same interview with Moyers, Armstrong addresses what in religion tries to curb that tendency in us to lash out against one another. She says that the spiritual practice that has the power to chip away at that destructive innate meanness in us is the practice of compassion.

Karen continues, "Compassion is not a popular virtue. Very often I talk to religious people and mention how important it is that compassion is the key, that it's the sine-qua-non of religion, people look kind of balked, and stubborn sometimes, as much to say, what's the point of religion if you can't disapprove of other people? And sometimes we use religion just to back up these unworthy hatreds, because we're frightened too. . . .

"There's great fear. We fear if we're not in control, other people will cut us down to size and so we hit out first. From the beginning violence was associated with religion but the advanced religions, and I'm thinking about Buddhism, Hinduism, the Hebrew prophets, they insisted that you must transcend violence, you must not give in to violence, but you must recognize that every person is sacred. . . ."

I agree with Armstrong that the need to control, to stay on top of things, in order to protect the "I" often brings out the use of force, in the myriad forms of diminishment and manipulation of others we use to keep people down, in check, within the confines of social control. If you can manage others' behavior to control their potential to create a threat or harm, maybe you can feel safer. But doing so doesn't respect people's sacred nature. Why not instead do what we've done intuitively? People liberated to devote themselves to helping rather than hurting, healing rather than destroying, seem to really like it. Under the right influences, as Tony puts it, "We're pretty good together."

"Compassion is hard," Karen says. "It's nothing to do with feeling. It's about feeling with others. Learning to put yourself in the position of the other person. There were years in my life when I was eaten up with misery and anger. I was sick of religion but when I got to understand what religion was really about, not about dogmas, not about propping up the church, not about converting other people to your wavelength, but about getting rid of ego and approaching others in reverence, I became much happier. . . ."

I'm happier too. I am so grateful to be part of such a profound opportunity. The School of Death is an incredible place to learn what Karen's talking about for real. I hear also from others who work in hospice ministries and chaplaincies to the dying who really identify with our work at Ground Zero—accompanying each other, people of all walks of life and many faiths, as we wrestle together with the great equalizer: death.

I wonder if Karen will be able to see how costly and difficult doing this has been? I hope she will connect what she is seeing with the religious journey she speaks about so movingly in her work. And that she will go and tell others outside this country, "This kind of spiritual awakening is happening in America. Do not be fooled by all the emphasis on retaliation you see on TV."

I do believe our country, despite some signs to the contrary, is on the road that Karen describes. I certainly feel that I am and that I am not alone. "You have to go a long journey that takes you away from selfishness and greed. And that leads you to value the sacredness in all others. I'm thinking of Abraham in Genesis—there's a wonderful story where Abraham is sitting outside his tent and it's the hottest part of a Middle Eastern afternoon, and he sees three strangers on the horizon.

"And now most of us would never dream of bringing a total stranger from the streets into our own homes, strangers are potentially lethal people. But that's exactly what Abraham does. He runs out, he bows down before them, as though they were kings, and brings them into his encampment, and makes his wife prepare an elaborate meal. And in the course of the ensuing conversation it transpires quite naturally that one of those strangers is Abraham's God. The act of practical compassion led to a divine encounter.

"In Hebrew the word for holy, *kadosh*, means separate, other. And sometimes it is the very otherness of the stranger, someone who does not belong to our ethnic or ideological, or religious group, an otherness that can repel us initially, which jerks us out of our habitual selfishness and gives intonations of the sacred otherness which is God."

The biblical story Karen tells is our story as well. It is both ancient and new. If we want to be the church in this strange new world, with all its new forms of lethal religious disapproval, fortified with weapons of mass destruction, and even using hijacked commercial airlines as agents of death, compassion is more important than ever. When we are inspired by that sense of reverence for all human life, acts of practical compassion can travel into even the most lethal places. We are free to do this. We can change the world, if we have the courage to enter the dark places of death, within and without our hearts, unarmed.

New Year's Eve is a turning point for the Little Chapel in more ways than one. On December 31, the rector of Trinity receives a letter from the Environmental Protection Agency (EPA) requiring that the roof of the chapel be cleaned of potentially toxic debris. It is decided that this is the warrant needed to insist on the chapel's closing. That will happen finally on Easter Day.

Lyndon has been worn down by constant pressure to agree to a closing date. He walks to the decisive meeting at Trinity, pauses, takes out a card from his breast pocket, and writes on its back, "I am a free man." But the arguments that most remains have been found by now in the site, combined with the EPA notice and request, lead him to capitulate in the end.

The staff accepts the news reluctantly. There is nothing we can do to object without being labeled insubordinate. I still don't quite believe it will happen although the handwriting is clearly on the wall. I'm probably in denial.

The rest of the world doesn't know this yet. And the crowds continue to come. As spring approaches the chapel enters a new season. It is a particularly poignant one for those of us who realize how few remaining days like these there are.

One in particular is the epitome of the final stage of our work. It is a beautiful spring day when a delegation of Japanese survivors of the atomic bomb from Hiroshima and Nagasaki come to visit St. Paul's.

Here they stand in an American church, having traveled across the world to say to us how sorry they are for our losses. That they know we are not cruel. It clearly brings them unspeakable joy to do this. They are offering to us the healing balm that absolves and forgives, renewing their own humanity and making us all one once more.

They come at the invitation of Colleen Kelly, a remarkable woman I have come to know and love. Colleen's younger brother, Billy, was attending a breakfast meeting in Windows on the World on 9/11. The family had no idea he was there. His office was in midtown. They were utterly shocked when they discovered his whereabouts that morning. They never saw Billy again and no remains have been found.

Colleen visits us regularly at the chapel and has become a good friend of the staff. She is a founding member of an organization called September 11 Families for Peaceful Tomorrows, another group who has begun to identify their purpose with the chapel's witness.

Peaceful Tomorrows is made up of family members of people who died in the Trade Center, in Pennsylvania, and in the Pentagon. They have come together to call for reconciliation rather than retaliation in the wake of 9/11. In January a group of its members courageously traveled to Afghanistan to bear condolences and assistance to Afghani families who have lost loved ones there in the bombings. They are, to me, representatives of the new church on the horizon, like us—part of that growing family that has formed a church of compassion in our hearts.

But Colleen and her colleagues have suffered the greatest loss and are even more willing to condole with strangers, daring even more bravely than we have ever dared to work in places visited by the lethal bent in humanity. On this day they are hosting the delegation from Japan at St. Paul's. I am completely in awe of all of them.

Colleen, who is Roman Catholic, has been helped greatly, she tells me, by an Anglican priest from South Africa, who has also served at St. Paul's. Michael Lapsley has come to the chapel, from halfway across the world, because his life's work is also about the kind of undefended healing compassion we are embracing. As one of the first white clerics in South Africa to join the African National Congress and publicly protest apartheid, Lapsley was sent a letter bomb that left him severely maimed, without hands and partially blind.

We hear at the service from Hidenori Yamaoka, who recalls being orphaned by the bomb. This painful childhood situation left a deep and lasting wound and caused him to hate the United States for over thirty years. Others describe the devastation of the aftermath. I have never heard people who experienced this describe what it was like—being one of the few left living in a sea of corpses, eating grass to survive.

The Japanese visitors and the grieving 9/11 family members talk with the recovery workers and hear their experiences in the pile. Together we prayerfully walk the chapel's cemetery. It is here that we are reminded that Hiroshima was the original Ground Zero.

The delegation recites their "Hiroshima-Nagasaki Message of Condolence":

> What you have done here is the perfect expression of the spirit of Hiroshima and Nagasaki, where so many survivors renounced revenge forever. Instead they worked ceaselessly against violence and for the world as a whole. We believe that we share with you the firm conviction that we must help the whole human race make a transition from a civilization of power to a civilization of love.

I can see in my mind's eye, Michael Lapsley, celebrating the noon Eucharist at the altar in St. Paul's. Lifting the consecrated host to God with two prosthetic hooks for hands, and praying:

> For in the night in which he was betrayed our Lord took bread. And when he had given thanks he broke it saying, "Take, eat. This is my body given for you. Do this in remembrance of me. Likewise after supper he took the cup, saying, "Drink you all of this. This is my Blood of the New Covenant, which is shed for you and for many for the forgiveness of sins. Do this as often as you shall drink it in remembrance of me.

And I hear in my ears the prayer of dismissal prayed by Lapsley and at the national interfaith service of mourning at the Washington National Cathedral immediately after the attack.

> Go forth into the world in peace; Be of good courage; Hold fast to that which is good. Render to no one evil for evil. Strengthen the faint hearted. Support the weak. Help the afflicted. Honor everyone. Love and serve the Lord.

It is in the spring, when so many great peacemakers and reconcilers of the world, whose vocations were forged in the fires of hate and cruelty, begin to come to the chapel, when I realize I too, in my own small way, am becoming one of those wounded healers. I don't see myself as unusual in any way. All of us in America now have that potential because of what we have experienced.

I believe that at least those of us who have spent this year living and working together came in part because of how hard we were fighting for our hearts—wanting to keep them soft and open and capable of kindness, and compassion and forgiveness, amid such paralyzing horror. Somehow we were given the grace to know instinctively that to do that we had to draw close to the suffering and be kind.

September 11 threw our lives out of balance and set us on a quest in search of what could restore a meaningful balance to our lives again. What we discovered is that kindness, given and received, was the only thing that could do that. Our hearts would always be restless until they rested in love.

I remember a conversation with Colleen, where in a moment of searing emotional honesty, talking about why she was going to Afghanistan, she broke down in tears and said, "Because I don't want to hate. I refuse to hate. I will not hate."

I am beginning to think the whole outpouring at St. Paul's can be read in a similar light. If we were completely frank I believe most of us would admit that part of the impulse to come and to serve others was to relieve the burden eating us inside. It is an unbearable, debilitating feeling to be consumed with fear, with terror, with anger, with bitterness. Even so we may nurse it, hold onto it, until something shakes up our perspective.

Paradoxically, feeling our own hearts turning to stone and experiencing the struggle to resist being hardened ourselves is sometimes the catalyst for feeling, truly feeling, compassion for our enemies. For the person who is struggling to keep their own heart soft now knows the battle of the heart that their enemy lost.

Then we know in our own hearts what is at stake, and say, "No more. Let the struggle and the healing begin with me." For as Desmond Tutu has often reminded the world, there is no future without forgiveness. We have to want the stray to come back.

———

In Lent the announcement is made to the congregation, the staff, all the volunteers and workers that St. Paul's will close on Easter Day. The timing is poor. The clearance of the pile is now hitting lower pockets, and contrary to previous predictions, the number of remains now being found increases sharply. Seven hundred are found in the bottom of an excavated elevator shaft in a single day. By this time nothing is recognizable.

We are all bone weary. Our emotional reserves for dealing with this are running very low. I haven't ever seen the workers look so depressed. People come from the pile catatonic from what they've encountered. As people sit in the chapel and unfreeze, or get into the food line, often they break down in uncontrollable sobs.

Lyndon begs the vicar to reconsider the closure given the fact that no one could have foreseen this turn of events. Thankfully he sees the pastoral issue and concedes it is worth careful consideration. But somehow this is not reported to the rector, and in an interview with the *New York Times* the vicar reports that cleaning plans remain as they ever were. Lyndon tells me on Palm Sunday, "Never have I identified so closely with Jesus. I feel like I'm riding on a slow donkey to my demise."

But on that same day an article comes out in Sunday's *New York Times* by a reporter named Tina Kelley. It gives me hope. She has done her research well and spoken to several of the workers. I've gotten wind ahead of time that the article will be printed, and rush to the newsstand Saturday night to wait for the first copy I can get my hands on. The first call I place is to Katherine, then Martin, and several others before the night is through. In each call we parse every sentence and debate whether it's really conceivable that Trinity will go through with shutting us down.

The most heart-wrenching elements of the article are the quotes from the workers about what the closing of the chapel will mean to them. Mike Bellone, an FDNY inspector, is quoted as saying, "We feel like we are being orphaned . . . how many bones and arms and hands can you pick up in a day before it gets to you? You come in here [the chapel] and they put a smile on your face. They help you keep your faith." Another firefighter, when asked what he plans to do when St. Paul's Chapel is closed, says, "I guess I'll go back to sleeping in my car." A third is quoted as saying, "Good things don't last anyway."

Rob Shwartz, a priest who was in the doctoral program at General with Lyndon and me and has been working in the morgue says, "This church has never been holier in its whole history. This is what it means to be a sacred place. To roll a stone in front of the tomb on Easter Sunday is just counter to what every church means to be."

The end of the ministry is starting to remind me of the beginning, as Internet and phone lines burn with alarm over the impending catastrophe. Letters and e-mails of protest pour in. Remaining neutral, simply repeating the party line, is the hardest thing professionally I have ever been called upon to do. Rumors of protests are flying. I am itching to join them. I hear that church members across the city are planning to picket Trinity throughout Holy Week. I can see NY1 cameras in front of the chapel interviewing workers for the news. Their comments are even more pointed than those quoted in the *Times*.

Fred relays an interview given by another fireman, John Misha, to a newspaper reporter from Dallas. Of all the comments to me it captures best the reality the workers are all trying to express.

"John Misha looked at the reporter and said, 'Lady, you know I'm a fireman right?' And she looked at him and shook her head yes. And then he said, 'Do you know what I do every day?' And she said, 'No.' And he said, 'Well I spend most every day on my hands and knees, digging with my bare hands for body parts.' And she was totally stunned. And then he went on to describe in the most vivid language the darkness and the suffering and the death. And then having watched her very carefully, and really laying it on her, suddenly his whole demeanor changed, and he stood ramrod straight, sucked in a whole chest of air, pushed out his chest, waved his hands in the air and said, 'And then I get to come in here.'

"Then standing in place and pointing around at every concession around all of St. Paul's, he talked about what the hospitality had meant to him. He said, 'Lady, I come in that door dirty, covered with blood, angry, pissed off and they hug me. They welcome me like I'm a real person. They treat me like a human being. And after that they hug me, they feed me, they massage me, they adjust me, they counsel me, and I sit here and listen to incredible music.' And he went on and on and on.

"He said, 'I bet you're Roman Catholic.' She said, 'Yes.' He said, 'So am I. But I come in here every day not just for the hugs and the food, but for the worship. This is where God is. These are my people. This is my new family. And this is the greatest sense of God's presence I have ever known.'"

At the same time all of this is happening, someone, I don't know who, picks up the phone and calls the New York City Department of Design and Construction, the city agency Mayor Giuliani has placed in charge of the recovery. This angel of mercy, whoever he or she is, asks if the department will intercede to request Trinity to allow the chapel to remain open.

On Monday we are sitting in my office when Lyndon receives an urgent call via two-way on his cell, to come to the vicar's office. When he arrives he is told that Trinity has decided to keep the chapel open.

I walk with Lyndon back to the chapel. A press release, we are told, is coming through the fax. We cannot even imagine what the response will be when Lyndon reads it to the assembled crowds. When we enter the church, Lyndon climbs the ladders to the top of the bell tower and rings the ancient bell. Then he scurries back and calls everyone together.

Everyone is holding their breath, waiting to hear what on earth the announcement will be now. Then Lyndon begins to read the release, "The Parish of Trinity Church today decided to continue its relief operation for workers at St. Paul's on Broadway."

Before he can read another word people go completely wild. We are screaming, cheering, clapping. A construction worker swings Katherine off her feet and twirls her around in the air. Police are kissing Grace. Everyone's hugging everyone. "Thanks be to God! Thanks be to God!" I can't stop praying those words.

We are not quite out of the woods. Later that afternoon I hear from Martin that a caveat has been delivered. The vicar wants the food operation to be shut down. But the angels of mercy are still looking over our shoulders. That very night Lyndon receives a call from Edwin Moore of the Federation of Protestant Welfare Agencies, who has been administering the *New York Times* Neediest Families Fund. They write a check for $200,000 to cover the food expenses from Easter until June.

This Easter Sunday is one where we surely feel the power of the Resurrection. There is a double baptism, the twin five-month-old daughters of a retired NYPD policeman. And yet, although the trees are beginning to bud and the grass to peek through the earth, it doesn't quite feel like spring. We have been at this for nearly seven months, and we are exhausted. We are also sad to be saying goodbye to Sister Grace, who is returning to her convent in Roxbury in just a few days.

Grace walks out into the cemetery to find a quiet moment for reflection. She says that she is feeling anxious and worried, wondering, "Will we ever heal from this tragedy? Will New Yorkers be okay? Will I?" She wanders under some trees and cannot believe that all these months later there is still debris above in the branches. But then she tells me she discovers something else.

"That's when I heard it. A rustling noise and a light and cheery chirp. It seemed to be coming from above me so I stopped and looked up into the gnarled old tree I had wandered under. This too had debris in it bunched up in half a dozen places where the branches were close together, like fingers that had reached out and grabbed their prize and were now unwilling to let go.

"To my astonishment those bits and pieces of debris had literally been transformed, made new, and were being used by the birds in their nests. In five separate spots in this tree and in two in the tree next to it the birds had built nests using bits and pieces of charred paper, tattered cloth, and twisted metal. Anything they could carry in their beaks they had used. They had taken the debris that had fallen out of the sky that horrible day and made it into building materials for their new homes. And you could hear the birds chirping to each other with joy. They had no idea this debris was from a tragic and destructive event. All they knew was that they had been given the building materials to use to build their nests—the safe places they would hatch and rear their young.

"I could feel the tears falling down my cheeks as I stood there in awe and wonder. I realized that somehow everything is going to be alright."

Slowly spring blossoms into a season of new birth. By the first of June the work is complete and it is time to say our goodbyes to one another. This is challenging. People are all saying, "How are we going to go on now? What are we going to do? I'm so used to coming here and now I can't anymore. It's all ending now and it's horrible."

But Ulla has a wise reply that I will hold in my heart and soul daily for the next four years.

"It is only an end if you see it as an end. But I would like to see it as a beginning. We've all been in training here, and we've had a very powerful training. It's as if we've been given a torch. Now we have to go out to the world, each to where we belong, and bring the torch with us. And take it from here to where it needs to go.

"Now we have to have the courage to move forward and move on and somehow allow the transformation to happen and translate all this into our lives in whatever form it needs to take. Let's allow the change. And let's allow the change to take place in the way it needs to take place. It might not be dramatic. It might be subtle. But let's not forget the lessons we learned from this. Let's not go back to where we were. There is no going back anyway."

# PART 2

# THE OTHER AMERICA

## CHAPTER 5

# THE DELUGE

THURSDAY, SEPTEMBER 1, 2005, IS A HOT AND STEAMY DAY IN NEW YORK City. I am standing in Villa Foyer with a CD called *Courage* in my hand. For the past year I have been editing hundreds of hours of taped interviews I conducted at Ground Zero, blending the voices of my beloved colleagues with meditations I have written on topics like "Sacrifice," "Forgiveness," and "New Birth." I open the jewel case adorned with an image of the distinctive red, white, and blue banner that became a symbol of the chapel and read the banner's quote painted in gold, "Courage is fear having said its prayers." I think to myself, "This whole project has been a kind of prayer."

The phone rings and I see on my cell it's Simon, my brother. He works for the producer of *Courage* and is no doubt calling to discuss some detail pertaining to the CD's launch. We've been straining to do this in time for the fourth anniversary of the attack—now ten days away. But like "The Shaping of Holy Lives," the film we were so excited to make with Rowan Williams on the day of 9/11, the launch of *Courage* is never to be.

I hear my brother's voice and can tell he is on speakerphone.

"Courtney," Simon says. "I am here in a meeting with the Episcopal Media Center's staff. I need you to sit down, take a deep breath, and listen to what we have to say."

Another member of the staff delivers the first part of the news. "Courtney, we're dropping the launch of *Courage*."

I have no idea what is coming next, but I can tell from their tone of voice I should brace myself. Another member of the staff continues.

"There is only one subject on the minds of the American people: 'what can we do for the victims of Katrina?' We want you to fly to Baton Rouge tomorrow. We'd like you to write, film, and narrate a ten- to fifteen-minute documentary within the next few days to tell churches what they need to do. Can you do that?"

A few hours later I hear from Peter Gudaitis, director of New York Disaster Interfaith Services. He reports to me that he will be leaving for Baton Rouge with the president of Episcopal Relief and Development (ERD) in the morning. Peter believes my experience with the St. Paul's ministry would be useful for the bishop of Louisiana to hear. He would like me to meet the new president of ERD, Rob Radtke, and is sure by connecting with the bishop I can gain access to what the church is doing on the ground for purposes of the film.

I call Skip Schueddig, the head of the Episcopal Media Center at home, and tell him I will be going to Louisiana at the crack of dawn. Then I call my brother to relay the news and ask him to meet me in Baton Rouge with the cameraman as soon as he is able.

In the early hours of the morning on September 2, as I turn out the lights in Villa Foyer, lock the door behind me, and step out into Fifth Avenue to hail a cab to the airport, I have the distinct feeling I may be saying goodbye to a whole era of my life. It is not a happy feeling. My mother has begged me on the phone, "Don't do this to yourself again." Her comment brings a tearful response that comes from my gut and surprises my brain.

"But, mother, all these years, I've tried so hard to stay faithful. Not to forget. Not to close up. If I don't go it means all that didn't really change me. I have to go, and I have to follow wherever this leads."

As the plane sails south in the pre-dawn hours, the voices on *Courage* fill my head and heart. Foremost is the memory of that first week at Ground Zero when we needed help so badly, and strangers came from everywhere, including Louisiana, uprooting their lives. Now, I realize it's simply my turn.

What I cannot imagine or conceive as I wing my way toward this disaster are the others who are living through these days from a plethora of histories and sightlines. Others who are, unbeknownst to any of us, on a converging path to form another uncanny American family, bringing heritage and history together in a combination and on a scale unlike anything any of us have seen or lived before.

Saundra Reed, a resident leader of the Central City community in New Orleans, is moving in with her family to the Baton Rouge home of her former college roommate, Bonnie. Already Saundra feels like she could talk for weeks on end about it all, and so far only a few days have passed since the storm. The mindset she held before Katrina hit seems like a perspective on life from the distant past, her thought process leading up to Katrina so innocent and naïve in retrospect. Now, looking back, Saundra reconstructs step by step what she did, what she thought, and why.

She explains, "Like everybody else in New Orleans, we all have our little routines and the way life goes. We handle extraordinary circumstances in a very routine kind of way.

"In my family there are five generations of us: My grandmother, my mother, and I. We have our children, and our children have their children. And really at one point we had six generations when my great-grandmother was with us. My grandmother probably has the most challenges because she has Alzheimers, but she also has a very good quality of life. It really wasn't hard to put her in the car. We just put her in the car and we go where we are going.

"But my daughter is on dialysis. And it's such a pain in the you-know-what to move her, to ride all these hours on the highway and not be in that community of understanding.

"So, I, in my infinite wisdom, I think I'm just going to get us a hotel room. The hotel will have generators and we'll be in a spot near Tulane University Hospital and we can just go there come Monday for her treatment.

"I couldn't find a hotel room in the city so I got one in New Orleans East. We had no idea this was the Big One. We had no concept of what that meant.

"So I went home and told everybody, 'Okay we're going to be in some hotel rooms in New Orleans East.' And my nephew said, 'Nanna, how could you? If we are going to be anywhere why would we be in New Orleans East? That's converted swampland.'

"I said, 'Well y'all didn't do anything.'

"So my good, good friend Linda Usdin called and said, 'What are y'all gonna do?' They were going to New York. So I told her about the hotel rooms and she said, 'Naw girl. I don't think y'all should do that. Why don't you go to our house in Poplarville, Mississippi?' We had gone to their property several times and it's really very, very nice. No radios. No televisions. Just a beautiful *On Golden Pond* kind of setting. And my kids of course were like, 'Yeah!' you know because it was like picnic time. So we decided we are going to Poplarville.

"On Saturday we head over to Walmart and Wally World is closing at four o'clock. That put the panic in me. When Walmart closes you need to be afraid. You need to be very, very afraid. We went to Walmart to get what we call our storm supplies, which is Oreos, raisins, sandwich meat, some extra water, some board games, and a few decks of cards. That's what it was, like that. A few candles too but none of that panic-kind-of-stuff.

"So we were going to leave the next day after church because we're all big churchers. We weren't going to run into the country and not even go to church on Sunday. That evening it got darker. And I kept saying, 'You know that highway's going to start to get closed.' So I'm thinking we might need to go before the highways get crowded. I say, 'Y'all wanta go tonight?' And everybody said, 'Yeah, let's go.' And it wasn't a panic yeah, it was an 'Oooh-one-more-day-in-the-country yeah. One extra day in this great place.' So we went to Poplarville. And it turns out that's where Miss Katrina went directly. It skimmed the city and went straight to Poplarville.

"So that Sunday morning we got up and the boys went fishin'. And they caught all these tremendous fish in this little pond. And we barbecued and we had a great day. And there's a pool there and everybody got in the pool. Okay so now we think we're going to batten down the hatches. And we listen to the radio, watched a couple of movies. We were fiddlin' while Rome was burnin'. It really was like that.

"So the evening came. Late the rain came. We lost power. Big deal we got candles. There were full windows from floor to ceiling and you could actually watch the storm outside. You could see the rain and the wind. Nothing came straight down. There were tall pine trees that were actually bending and I kept hearing that old spiritual, 'Green trees a-bendin'. Sinner, why you stand there tremblin'?' Because they would actually bend down and after a while you saw them go snap, snap, snap, snap. They just broke in half.

"But like the song says, 'An evil shall not come nigh my dwelling.' Trees fell. A big, *he-uge* magnolia tree in the back yard just tipped over like an old lady with her skirt up. Nothing hit any of our cars. Nothing hit any of the buildings. But it was just . . .

"At one point, we heard this creaking sound and it was actually the bookshelves on the window wall. And the reason it was creaking was because the wall had begun to tilt in, the wind was just that strong. So we had a bench that went with a long, long grand dining table. And we had to prop it against the wall because the whole world was coming in. It was one of the scariest . . . no, it was *the* scariest moment of my lifetime. We had no water. We had no power. We no longer had radio coverage and we had no phone because all the towers were down.

"In the morning we sent some of our young men out to the highway. Now Poplarville, Mississippi, in order to go wherever we were, you had to go off the main road, down a side road to a path, then down the path to a trail. It was like that. So we sent some of the boys out to see what was goin' on. Because we couldn't get off the property. The trees were almost like they were thatched. Though none of our cars were disabled we couldn't move them. So the boys did the Grizzly Adams thing—made a little trail—because my daughter needed her dialysis. And when they got to the road and were able to attract the sheriff he said there was nothing he could do to get her to a hospital.

"Now I know she's going to fill up. But if she wasn't really bleedin' and it wasn't life threatening they were not taking us anywhere. So we ended up trekking out to the highway. Getting my sister's SUV and driving over some stuff that wasn't meant to be driven over and driving all the way to Jacksonville to get her dialyzed. So our party separated for us to do that for the first time. They were praying everything was okay with us, and we were praying everything was okay with them—thirteen people and three dogs altogether.

"Then in Jacksonville we are where we can get communication and we finally know what is happening. We bought groceries and headed back. So when we get back to Poplarville everyone is asking us, 'When are we going to be able to go home?' And we had to share with the family, 'We have no home. There is nothing.'

"I called my college roommate. She was in Baton Rouge and she was ecstatic to hear from us because she couldn't reach anybody. And I said, 'I don't know where we're gonna go or what we're gonna do.' And she said, 'You're gonna keep driving till you get to my front door and I'm gonna be standing there when you get here.'

"I can't tell you. We didn't have nowhere to go. The only us there was was us, you know? Nobody. Nobody. Nobody had any idea what this meant. We didn't know. Imagine you walk through the door and you turn around to say something to somebody inside and you look back over your shoulder and all that's there is the edge of a cliff. There is nothing that you knew, and there is no way you can walk back. You can't retrace your steps. There is nothing you can go back and get to facilitate the steps going forward. There is only wilderness in front of you.

"We got little kids. We got dogs. We got old people with infirmities. We have to feed them. There is no electricity. We can't even get to whatever money we had because we can't do nuthin' with electronic cards. We think, 'They have to hurry up and do somethin' about it.' We didn't even know who the hell 'they' were. And they were in as bad a shape as we were in.

"People use the word *devastation* and I take issue with that. This was not devastation, it was decimation. It was Hiroshima. Nagasaki. It was that. It was that. Every network. Every connection was completely gone.

"My dear, dear Katrina angel Bonnie, my former college roommate, is a very practical woman. She was really, really most kind. But she was trying to give me some tough love two or three days into this and Bonnie said, 'You know, I'm not going to judge anybody but people in New Orleans tend to stay in New Orleans and they never ever go away. They don't do that a lot so this is very scary for a lot of people because they've never even thought of wanting to go anyplace else. People are going to have to get comfortable with the fact that they are going to have to go on in another place.'

"'But,' I said to her, 'that's home. You lose your orientation when you don't have home. You kind of set your plumb line.' And Bonnie said, 'It's superficial to think about Mardi Gras and the French Quarter and that kind of riotous living as your plumb line. It's just that you've been socialized that way for a long time.'

"I almost lost my best friend that day. I decided to be really quiet because I was listening to her perspective. And it was an outside-in perspective. And because I love her and she loves me back, I knew she was speaking out of turn but it was from a loving a place.

"And I said to Bonnie, 'You know, people who live in New Orleans don't even get up for that kind of hype. Understand this. This is a loss, a loss like losing your parents and your children all at the same time. It's like Lot's loss. We've lost our memories. We've lost our connectivity—one of the most important valuable pieces we own as New Orleanians is our familialness, the fact that we know we have that zero degree of separation. Now we don't have our linkages that make us who it is that we are.'

"Folks don't understand this about New Orleans. If I am on any corner and in trouble I will never feel lost or unattended to for more than fifteen minutes. Somebody that I know is gonna pass and see about me. If there is a problem in terms of health, home, heart, healing, education—I don't care what part of my life it is—I know who to go to. I don't have that anyplace else in the whole wide world. This is a loss I can't even describe and unless you look at it like that you can't understand it."

Saundra continues, "I was a food stamp and welfare supervisor at that time. So the day after I got to Baton Rouge I went to the food stamp office. I went down and everybody I knew in the New Orleans office all said we're going in to help.

"We went to work. We sometimes worked from six in the morning. And it was therapy for me to be of service.

"I understood personally that it was such a hard thing, our elders, our people who worked, who did all kinds of professional work, and now they were just hangin' on by the skin of their teeth. None of us could afford to say to ourselves, 'I'm a helper. I'm not the helped!'

"And finding myself in that position of need was very, very hard. As a single mom, with a prideful spirit, I had never received any food stamps or any welfare the whole time I raised my children. I had to recognize I was struggling to receive help because of a prideful spirit. I had never thought about it like that because I was comfortable thinkin' that my good deeds I was doing for others were for the lesser people. I was approaching that work and thinking of that work from a very prideful place. I was.

"I raised my family without food stamps, but now I am seeing I don't get a red badge of courage for that. That was a profound understanding for me. It leveled me out to realize that part of me. I didn't like that about me but it was real.

"Now I wanted to be able to say to other people who were proud in shame that you know, that's what this was made for. It was made for an emergency situation. Because it was hard for people to accept public benefits in a charity mode.

"On top of that it was becoming apparent we were going to have to fight for our assistance. The Red Cross was giving out some aid, but on purpose they said they were not going to say where they were giving out assistance or how much assistance it was. They said they were doing it that way because they did not think they were going to be able to handle the crowd that was going to come. Now how horrible is that?

"Then, as I stood out in a line on Airline Highway waiting to apply, I said to the man who was policing the line, 'I have my mother's and my grandmother's information. Will they be entitled to benefits? Will I be able to take care of them?' And he said, 'No, they are going to have to come.' And I said, 'My grandmother is ninety-five. My mother is seventy-five. You mean to tell me they are going to have to come stand out here in this heat?' He said, 'I just know they are not going to let you handle more than your own case.'

"There was nobody we could trust to fill in. We heard the government and at first it sounded like they were giving us an answer we could live with. Very quickly we found out it was all smoke and mirrors. So we discovered America. We found out. And what we saw was not pretty.

"It's been a lie for a long, long time. It's been a lie that we didn't know about. The government would rather do anything but look at the lie. The truth about it is not a simple truth. Economic disparity and prejudice is real on so many levels it's like an onionskin.

"But I believe we all have our spiritual gifts. And mine is helps and exhortations. In every phase of my life and every part of my character it's helps and exhortations. Now I see, in this desolate place, my natural bent for advocacy is important because we need advocates on our behalf. When you are so wide-eyed and scared about where your next breath or meal or shelter is coming from it's very difficult for people to say, 'Naw you can't do me like that.'

"I've met with Mary Joseph from Children's Defense Fund and Linetta Gilbert from the Ford Foundation. We've talked about how we might need to get out of the way and look over our shoulders and look at the next generation of leadership coming up. We've said, 'Maybe there is somebody else coming up behind us who is going to do the job that we were supposed to do.' Not just the articulate and educated voices of some of our young people, but the raw urban outcry of the young people we have failed."

In a townhouse in the suburbs of Charlottesville, Virginia, a semi-retired fifty-four-year-old black activist named Shakoor Aljuwani, son of a Mississippi sharecropper, veteran of the steel mills of Buffalo, New York, is watching the television. He has moved to Virginia recently, after a lifetime of working in some of the toughest neighborhoods in America. He has decided to take a break from organizing block-clubs, fighting to revive depressed, low-income black and Latino communities, and is working on a book. It is about the failures of leadership he has witnessed in the black community since his days in civil rights and the Black Nationalist movement.

He is glued to the screen and he is angry. His wiry frame will not sit still. All he sees is pain—desperate men and women trapped on rooftops day after day—and the same maddening clip looped over and over again of a handful of people looting a store. It is driving him crazy. He is pacing the house cursing the TV. This must be selective reporting. Where are the heroic deeds he knows are there?

His partner Barbara Ehrenreich, a well-known author and activist herself, suggests, "Shakoor, why don't you do something about it? I'm afraid if you don't this TV may soon be destroyed."

The two begin to discuss what "doing something" might mean. The conversation shifts to Ben, Barbara's son, and a reporter for *L.A. Weekly* assigned to write a set of stories in New Orleans. Barbara is concerned about her son's safety. Perhaps if Shakoor met Ben in New Orleans, two dilemmas could be solved. Shakoor could help Ben find stories that break the enraging stereotypes, and mom might worry less about her son's security. It sounds like a good idea to Shakoor. Because black males are having a particularly hard time entering the city, they work it out that Shakoor will impersonate Ben's photographer.

The next day Shakoor flies to Houston where he and Ben rent a car and begin their drive to New Orleans. In the car they talk about what they have seen on TV. They want to get underneath the stories blanketing the airwaves and find some of the spontaneous grassroots neighborhood responses that are undoubtedly saving lives. As they are entering the city they hear Governor Blanco issue her "shoot to kill" order broadcast on the radio.

They move into the Sheraton on Canal Street. Not a room. There are no rooms. All the windows in the hotel are blown out. The press corps is camped out in a lounge adjacent to the bar on the hotel's third floor. Everyone is sleeping on the floor. They try to find bathrooms that don't make you sick to enter. Each finds a spot in the corner of the carpeted room to sleep. Some of the more established media outlets arrive with MREs (meals ready to eat). Everyone is sharing food.

Of the many stories they hear, Shakoor is particularly moved by his encounter with a Korean War veteran named James. They meet at the St. Claude Bridge crossing into the Lower Ninth when James, a large man in his late sixties, emerges from the water pulling a little luggage carrier packed with all he has left to his name. Shakoor walks over, gives him some water and energy bars, the first food this survivor has eaten in days.

James lived in the Lower Nine. On Monday morning he woke to the sound—boom! He can see from the window of his house that the levee wall has breached and water is gushing through. James goes quickly to the attic of his one-story house, grabs his axe and hacks a hole in the roof to climb through. The roof is not high enough. The whole house is already submerged and water is sweeping him off his feet. James swims to a tree and grabs a branch where he holds on for the better part of a day. People are shouting from higher rooftops and other treetop branches. They are shouting words of encouragement so that those they can see around them won't give up and let go.

For hours James watches neighbors float by—dead. He is trying to swim out and catch and secure some of the bodies so he can bring them to a decent resting place when the water subsides. He succeeds in holding onto an old woman's body in the tree for several hours before losing the strength. It does something to him when he has to let her go.

It is unbearably hot. The decomposing bodies littering the streets are the hardest part to stomach. They are not only in the eastern part of town. They are uptown too—on formerly swanky, oak-lined St. Charles Avenue, on the lower part of the previously bustling commercial area of Magazine Street. At the corner of Magazine and Jackson Avenue, Shakoor and Ben are some of the first to identify the corpse of an old black woman. Citizens are beginning to construct her grave.

There is an old black man standing in a gas station across the street. He looks like a lot of folks—shell-shocked, dazed. Shakoor goes over to the car while Ben is taking photos of the body and writing down the epitaph. As Shakoor hands over some water and energy bars he tries to engage the man in conversation but it's hard. Blank stares and nods are the only responses the man can summon.

**The Site Reclaimed:
What Faith Can Do.**

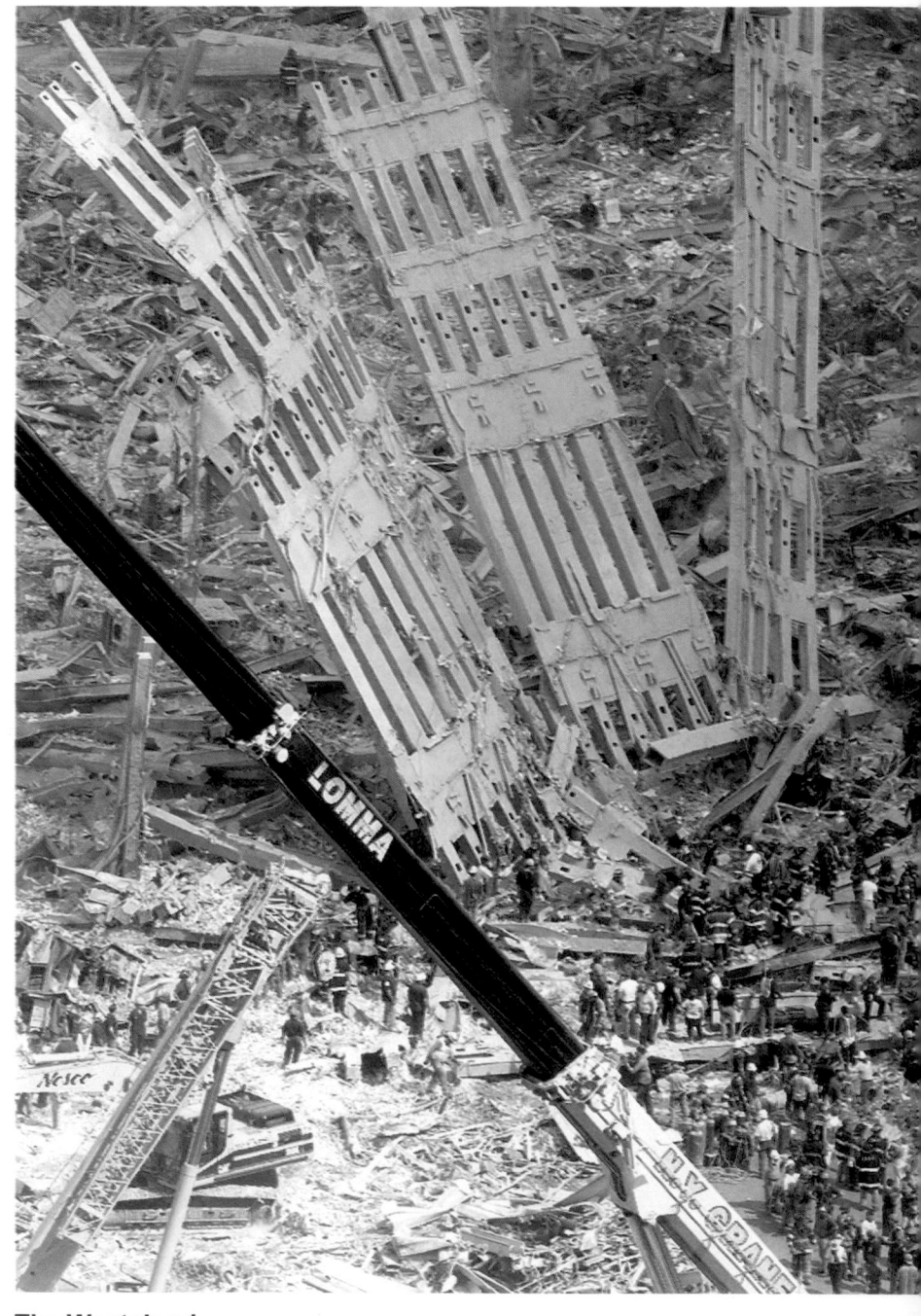

**The Wasteland** RUTH FREMSON OF THE *NEW YORK TIMES*

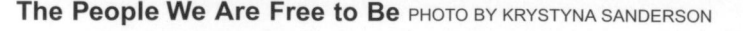

**The People We Are Free to Be** PHOTO BY KRYSTYNA SANDERSON

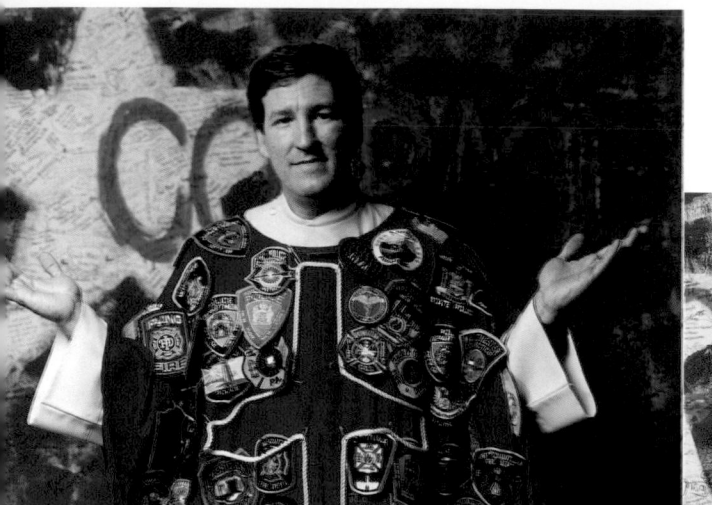

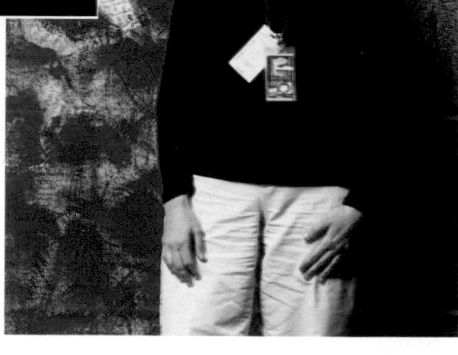

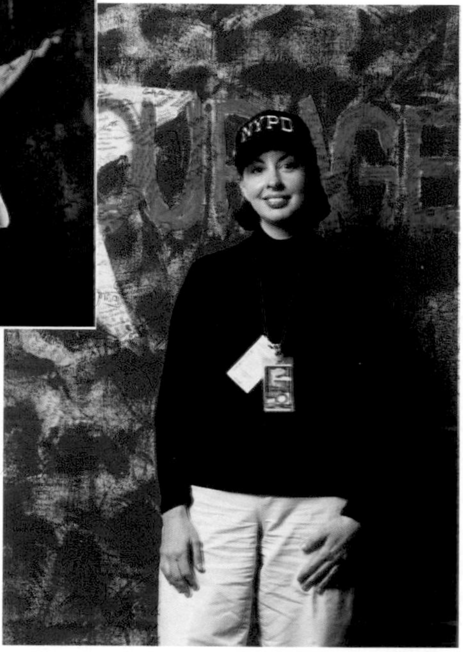

Above: Lyndon Harris. "It's quite natural to have fear but we are called to a different place."

Right: Courtney Cowart. "The work kept my heart open and that's what I really wanted—was to live my life with that kind of open heart."

Below left: Jimmy Abbananto and Jerry Krusch. "Most cops don't get to bond with people. This is good."

Below right: Katherine Avery. "We've created a space where people give sacrificial-ly—where we feel free to do that."

KRYSTYNA SANDERSON (ALL PHOTOS ON THIS PAGE)

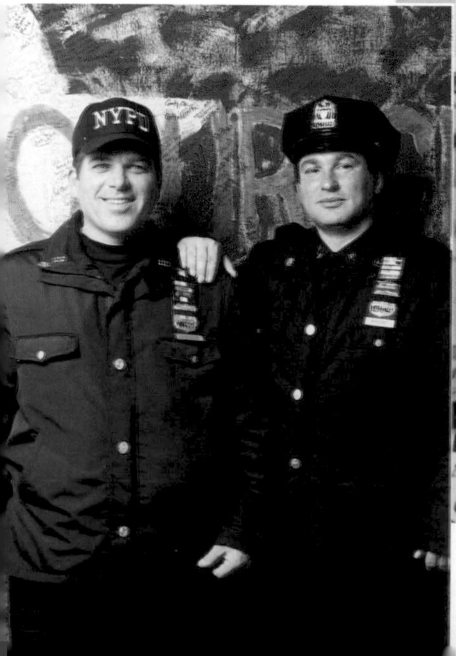

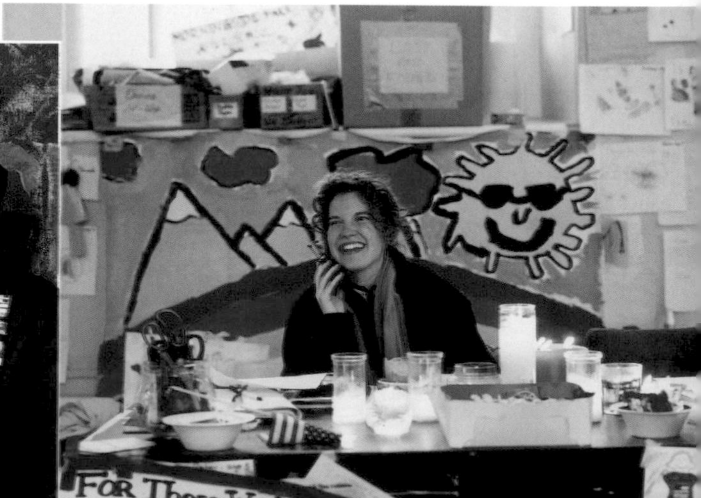

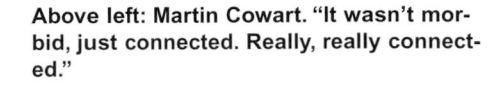

Above left: Martin Cowart. "It wasn't morbid, just connected. Really, really connected."

Above right:Sister Grace. "I could feel the tears falling down my cheeks as I stood there in awe and wonder. Somehow everything was going to be alright."

Left: Joe Bradley. "I never thought I'd have a family like this one."

Below: Fred Burnham (with Lyndon Harris and Courtney Cowart). "We discovered the emotional magnificence of life."

KRYSTYNA SANDERSON (ALL PHOTOS ON THIS PAGE)

## Diverse Prayers

KRYSTYNA SANDERSON
(ALL PHOTOS)

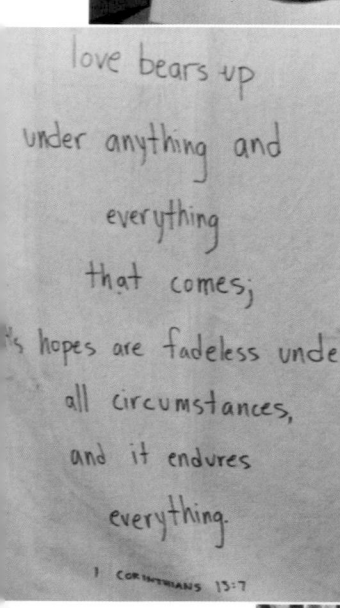

love bears up
under anything and
everything
that comes;
it's hopes are fadeless under
all circumstances,
and it endures
everything.

1 CORINTHIANS 13:7

# The Raw Outcry of the Children We Have Failed

**Fyre Youth "Take It To the Top" on the steps of the Louisiana State Capitol.**
JIM BELFON. GULF SOUTH PHOTOGRAPHY PROJECT

**Shakoor Aljuwani (center) stands with youth at protest before the Board of Elementary and Secondary Education in Baton Rouge.** JIM BELFON. GULF SOUTH PHOTOGRAPHY PROJECT

The Walk Begins

Bishop Charles Jenkins joins our Central City neighbors in the Silence Is Violence march.

Left: The Work Begins

Below: Louisiana Gothic

**Youth of America
Answer the Call**

## Youth of New Orleans Answer the Call

**Above: If a kid has a horn in his hand he won't have a gun.**

**Right: Carolyn Lukensmeyer of America*Speaks* honors the youth of *To Be Continued* at Community Congress II.**

**Below: *To Be Continued* Brass Band second-lining to register neighbors for Community Congress II.**

JIM BELFON. GULF SOUTH PHOTOGRAPHY PROJECT

## The Strength of the Community

**Above: Our mentor, Gus Newport, former mayor of Berkeley, California (right), with Roger Clay (left) of the National Economic Development and Law Center, Oakland, California.** JIM BELFON. GULF SOUTH PHOTOGRAPHY PROJECT

**Right: Our hero, Big Shed. Saving lives one poem at a time.**

**Below: Our leader, Bishop Charles Jenkins with The Most Rev. Rowan Williams, Archbishop of Canterbury proclaiming the dignity of every human being.** GEORGE LONG

# The Questions of the Community

The day of the Jena March Cha'von asks Archbishop Rowan: Why can't people just get along?

**Archbishop Rowan answers: We have to help people feel safe.**

## The Hope of the Community

**Above: Obama—Our struggles are heard.** SHAKOOR ALJUWANI

**Right: Princess—a straight-A student.** GEORGE LONG

**Below: The Community Congress—Let us agree to a shared fate.** JIM BELFON. GULF SOUTH PHOTOGRAPHY PROJECT

All of a sudden a dark Chevy Suburban swings into the gas station. The tinted windows are partially lowered and automatic weapons are sticking out of the side. They practically run Shakoor and the old man over. Two young men in black jump out. Shakoor immediately checks their chests for tags. Are they New Orleans police? Sheriffs? New York police? Fish and Wildlife? All these groups are in the city. In fact so many different law enforcement jurisdictions are here it has become a reflex when somebody approaches to figure out first who they are. Then you can gauge how they might treat you.

But these guys don't have anything on them. No tags. No badges. Just black pants and black t-shirts with a little word printed on the left side on the chest over an insignia that says "Blackwater." At this point one guy comes over and points his rifle at Shakoor.

"What's the problem?" Shakoor asks. He starts to add "officer" and then he stops and says, "Who are you? What are you? What is Blackwater? What is your problem? We're not doing anything. What's your problem?"

The mercenary's answer is to push Shakoor in the chest with the butt of the gun. The older man, already traumatized, is growing increasingly agitated. Shakoor is backing up, his hands in the air, saying over and over again, "Look, everything is okay. I don't understand. What's the problem?" Then the man with the gun makes Shakoor get on his knees. The other guy makes the older man get on his knees. They are putting the tips of their rifles to the backs of their heads—execution style.

Suddenly Ben is running across the street yelling, " *L.A. Weekly*! *L.A. Weekly*! This is my cameraman. What are you doing?" The two men in black look over their shoulders at Ben, waving his press pass, running flat out. They kick Shakoor to the ground, and then before Ben can reach them, jump in the vehicle and speed off. Ben runs down Jackson Avenue behind the SUV yelling, "Who are you? I want an explanation!" but to no avail.

That night back at the Sheraton a lot of the long-term veteran press, who know each other from Afghanistan, Iraq, difficult parts of Africa, are in tears, frustrated, astounded. They listen to Shakoor's story with grave concern. They have been investigating other stories: six black men have been shot by authorities on the Mississippi River Bridge simply for trying to walk into un-flooded Algiers. There are reports of other young black males being shot by authorities and thrown in the river or left by the side of the road. The reporters are all saying they are filing these stories but they aren't being run. Ben, in fact, is the only one who writes a story on these events that sees the light of day.

The tone of conversation among the press is one of universal amazement. Everyone is trying to figure out, "What happened? How did we go from helping people survive to seeing ordinary civilians as a threat? How did this happen—this abuse on top of abuse?" The air is full of fear, and the greatest fear is there is no law.

That night Shakoor lies on the floor of the Sheraton staring at the ceiling. He is talking to himself loudly in his head. "This is insane. The authorities have turned everything upside down. How do I get control of myself so I don't lose it? Clearly demanding your rights is not the thing to do. That will get you killed."

"Now," Shakoor thinks to himself, "you understand how your parents and your grandparents felt. Why they functioned the way they did. Why they didn't stand up and say, 'You can't treat me like that.' When you were a kid you never understood. But now you understand.

"When all the power—the police, the military—is against you, for you to survive you have to pick your battles. You have to prostrate yourself when you should be standing up for your rights so that you will be alive to speak up another day. You never thought you'd be in that position, but if you are going to make it through you better understand that now. You don't have any rights down here. You have to take note of that and wait for a better day to fight. Or else you could be erased and nobody would ever know. Nobody would be able to do a single thing about it."

The next day Shakoor and Ben ride through the city again. They are struck by the way the youth of the city are caring for the city's abandoned elders. They go out through the streets collecting those stranded, gathering them on a porch or any dry place they can find, forage for food, bringing supplies back to help the seniors. Guarding their safety at night. Encouraging them to hold on.

One older group of five they assist all are diabetic and three are insulin dependent. They haven't had insulin in days. Shakoor and Ben find National Guard and convince them to come back and give these stranded people a ride to a place they can receive treatment before some of them die.

Eventually Shakoor and Ben find a group that has gathered around a longtime New Orleanian named Malik Rahim. Malik's group doesn't have gasoline, but they are delivering water to seniors on bicycles. Shakoor and Ben put their truck at the disposal of the volunteers and make deliveries throughout the day. At suppertime Shakoor meets another crew of remarkable black youth.

This is a group of New Orleans teens that is showing particular courage and ingenuity. Some have commandeered abandoned city buses and driven routes to collect stranded families until their vehicles run out of gas. Another group has hijacked Brown's Dairy's milk trucks to save people from dire circumstances. Another has made a raft out of tires. All spend their days rescuing life: diving off the I-10 overpass and swimming to pull people out of the water, to pull people off of rooftops, transporting the sick and dying to medical assistance.

One finds a person with a baby who needs Pampers. Another baby needs formula. Another person needs shoes—they ran out with bare feet and now their cuts are becoming infected from the polluted water. The young men compile their lists. They don't take anything they don't need. Given the shoot-to-kill order issued by the Governor they are risking their lives to do this. But something is more important than their individual survival. What they are doing is the only thing keeping babies and seniors alive.

On their last night in the city, Shakoor makes a promise to Malik that although he is leaving the next day, he will be back. He returns to Virginia haunted. He begins to dream about the heroic youth he saw and heard. He feels like he has abandoned them and knows he cannot live with himself if he does not return. Over and over he pictures the courage. That is what is so powerful. That is what must be supported. As crazy as it seems, after nearly losing his life, New Orleans is the place he wants to be.

He walks into the room to tell Barbara. "I've drawn my line in the sand. I'm going back to volunteer."

Shakoor is used to being in a very small minority of folks who care about the suffering of impoverished African Americans—a handful of voices in the wilderness. But it is becoming clear that many eyes have been opened wide.

For example, Shakoor and Barbara's next-door neighbor is an ex-Marine. The night this interracial couple moved into their house the neighbor had some issues. There had been low-level tension for about a year.

When Shakoor returns the neighbor hears he has been in New Orleans and invites him over. Shakoor thinks it's going to be terrible, a very short conversation, and he'll be thrown out of the neighbor's house. But within fifteen minutes the Marine and his wife are in tears. "I can't believe we treated Americans like that," the soldier says. Shakoor tells him the story of the Korean War veteran, and the Marine has to walk out of the room. He comes back in and says, "I am so ashamed."

The Marine begins to raise money to help send Shakoor back to the city. And whenever he sees Shakoor's car in the driveway he puts a little note on the windshield, "I've got some Guinness. Come on over and tell me what we need to do."

The Marine cannot believe that Shakoor, on his own with a trunk load of water, beat the U.S. military to the point of need. That garners the soldier's respect and friendship forever. He and Shakoor discover they share a genetic code that says when people are in need we rise up to help them and that trumps everything else.

Shakoor is thinking hard and it seems to him when a country really hits this kind of earth-shattering disaster, it changes who we are. People can make that shift and make it in a massive way. And that hope, that possibility, is why he is going to New Orleans to serve.

Across the globe in Nigeria, a thirty-year-old New Orleanian named Nell Bolton is working with Catholic Relief Services on justice, peace building, and good governance projects throughout Central Africa. She has worked in Africa for two years, working with grassroots organizations to ensure oil and gas revenues accrue to the benefit of local people. She has worked side by side with relief workers putting their lives on the line, with colleagues who have been arrested and perpetually harassed by the government. She has come to know what working as an outsider but in solidarity with local people in a place of violence, injustice, and poverty really means.

On the night of August 29 Nell watches the CNN reports. Thankfully, the word is that New Orleans has dodged the bullet. On Tuesday morning her relief is reversed when Nell goes to work and begins to read the blogs with eyewitness accounts of the levees breaking. Immediately her heart sinks. She understands the implications of this, long before the newscasters understand, before alarms make their way through the international press.

It is a very lonely period of fear and grief. No one around Nell has any way of understanding what this means to her. In Nigeria loss and suffering is ubiquitous. Nell feels as great a tragedy as this is to her, it will never compare with the daily loss and suffering of Nigerians. She has no support group and no network of others feeling what she is feeling.

On Wednesday night Nell is in tears, alone, so far away. She is weeping over the pain, feeling the suffering of the people of her city combined with her own hurt. It feels like a tremendous unmooring. She can't do anything. She can't touch anyone. She can't see anything for herself. The helplessness is also intensified by the fact that she is living without connections, living without family, so far away.

By the fifth day after the storm Nell decides she is moving home. It is something she knows with perfect clarity, although the details of how she will do this are not yet evident. What she feels is a call.

She is thinking to herself, "If New Orleans is home, if you really believe that and you don't go home and help rebuild and recover, what does it mean to be from that place? What does it mean to be connected to a people? What does it mean to have roots if at this time when the city is in such need you are not willing to be a part of that experience?"

She is also thinking, "Can you with any integrity continue to work on good governance in other parts of the world when we so clearly don't have a handle on this at home? New Orleans is a place you know. It's a place you are connected to. You've done this in a place where you are an outsider, now it is time to be an insider again. Both worlds are valuable, but now it is time to go home."

It has been a big shock seeing what Nell has seen, even from a distance. There is a need, almost like the need after a physical blow, to pat down your body and make sure all your parts are there. It is a powerful need to return and see with her own eyes, and touch with her own hands, the community where she was born and raised.

The question is where to begin to search for a niche. Trinity Episcopal Church is a starting place. It is where Nell's faith was nurtured growing up. The church's school is where Nell was educated. Nell's aunt is senior warden of the church, a logical person to ask, "What does Trinity want to do?"

Nell knows she wants to be part of seeking reconciliation—seeking social healing in the city. That's her background, her discipline, what she went to graduate school to study. She knows Trinity is a congregation with an anti-racism commitment. Although she hasn't lived in New Orleans for six years, and in some ways will have to start from scratch, Trinity seems like a logical foothold.

Nell requests a leave to go home to New Orleans for a week. After chatting with the new rector for all of fifteen minutes, the priest cuts to the chase. "How much will we need to pay you?" The transition home is happening fast, but there is a sense of total integrity at the core of her being about this choice.

At home, on her short visit back, Nell finds the newspaper makes her cry every day. There are so many heartbreaking stories, so many landmarks lost, the loss of so many people's histories. But because of her life experience in Nigeria, decimated New Orleans feels familiar. This part is a surprise. The huge amounts of devastation, the stench, the mountains and mountains of debris, the lack of electricity, water, telephones—these are all the conditions she's grown accustomed to in Africa. What is tremendously difficult for Americans has for Nell become a way of life. In a strange way she thinks it will make the transition back to this country easier.

Because Nell did not lose anything personally she does not feel it is her place to say out loud to people, "Count your blessings. This is how nine-tenths of the world lives." But inside she believes that in the pain and suffering there is a blessing for us. It is a blessing she hopes at the right point in the grieving process can be acknowledged collectively and one day lifted up.

The way Nell sees it, "New Orleans has been given a precious gift. So few Americans ever have the experience of the reality of the precariousness of life, and the strength of life at the same time. That precariousness is what most people in the world live. That is the world. That is real." She hopes to play a role in connecting the people of the city with that reality so that New Orleanians can "be in solidarity in better ways, living not as most Americans live in the illusion, but to live from a faith perspective, recognizing we are not in control."

Nell journals, "We struggle so much to let go and let God—to trust God. We have so little in our normative daily American culture that reinforces that struggle and helps us get to that place. We all experience death and loss and bereavement, but this kind of collective catastrophic loss is a different reference point for struggle. In this context there are so many more opportunities to get to that point of trust in God.

"And what do we do with those opportunities? For me it's a hope that out of this, we as a city, as a community, as a country will come to a place of expanded compassion. We have the opportunity to transcend the frustrations, and the roadblocks, and the pressures we face, and focus on replicating throughout our whole community generous hearts, and generous spirits. It can come out of the way we live. It can come through the way we live, and if we live compassionately I believe that will expand compassion."

Two months later Nell Bolton is packing her bags in Africa and traveling back home to Louisiana permanently to try to live compassionately and to support the expansion of compassion in all of us.

The Episcopal Bishop of Louisiana, Charles Jenkins, is standing at a window on the second floor of St. James Church in Baton Rouge, wearing a pair of borrowed khakis rolled up at his ankles and belted high above his waist. His house on the lake in Slidell is probably gone, and he has no idea of the condition of any of his southern Louisiana churches. The window is where he stands to try to get a cell phone signal. The communications grid in Baton Rouge has collapsed. The cell phone usually doesn't work, but has in one case—the call placed to Rob Radtke, president of Episcopal Relief and Development, pleading for help. Now Rob and Peter Gudaitis have arrived.

Already their perspective has been an enormous help. With the bishop they have visited the Baton Rouge River Center, a huge convention complex filled with 14,000 evacuees. Peter and Rob have been appalled by what they see and are working the phones to pull together an emergency meeting of ecumenical leaders and response directors for a chat concerning what to do to make the shelter more humane.

Peter is outraged by the lack of sensitivity in the way the River Center is being run. Here are thousands of people who have been through unspeakable trauma. Now they are being assaulted by do-gooders, Scientologists, and the press. Gudaitis has made an observation to the bishop that is seared in Charles Jenkins's mind: "The people here don't even have the right to say, 'I don't want a massage.' We're going to do something about this. These reporters are not going to come through and flash their grief."

It makes an impression on the bishop. He thinks to himself Peter is right about the level of intrusiveness the people are enduring. "Here are folks who have absolutely no control over anything in their life—even to the point of saying who can or cannot touch them." That is the first moment that the violation of human dignity as the chief moral issue and spiritual sin uncovered by the floodwaters of Katrina, a matter even more pressing than the question of survival, comes to Bishop Jenkins. Peter Gudaitis has given him eyes to see.

Night comes. The bishop is staying in the house of a friend on the outskirts of Baton Rouge. He cannot wipe one image in particular, of all the images of degradation, from his mind. As he hears the rhythm of helicopters hovering overhead, airlifting more and more stranded survivors from the toxic waters, he thinks of the scene that particularly moved and still haunts him. It is the image of an aged African American woman standing in front of the New Orleans Convention Center. She is holding a hand-written sign that says, "I am an American too." As she stands there in front of the television camera, an army truck loaded with water drives past her. Jenkins thinks to himself, "This is what we have done."

The bishop is reeling at the size of the sin. The response to this that the body of Christ must make . . .

Days after Katrina, he calls this night his "Dark Night of the Soul."

Two and a half years later, the bishop borrows a term from Rabbi Jonathan Sachs to explain the source of his of agony: "Their fate is our fate. We share a common fate." He sees what the church's response must be, but he feels he is incapable of making or leading that response.

"I did not have the capacity, the experience to respond to this as a Christian. Here I am from an agricultural family in north Louisiana, raised in an atmosphere of prejudice and separation. My first play-mates were African Americans. At a certain age you learned you didn't do that. The Klan threatened both my grandparents at one time or another for actions or in-actions. We were slightly different but still part of that racist society. The response that the body of Christ needed to make now was so far beyond my past, my experience, my capability. All I could do was pray. I was very fretful and fearful.

"I called our diocesan treasurer, who would not identify himself in any way, shape, or form as a Christian hero. But he came over and helped calm me down, and he promised that he and many others would stand with me.

"So I prayed that night that God would give me grace, and a strength and a vision that was far beyond myself, and I do believe in the reality of prayer. I did not realize that night the crosses I would get that would come along with that grace. I did not realize that. But I think the prayer was the right thing to ask.

"I would say to anyone else when you ask those things—when you've been brought so low that all you have is what is in one suitcase—and you pray for the gifts of leadership and wisdom, with those gifts come crosses so that you do not become overly confident in yourself. They continually come and become less frightening but no less painful. But that is the opportunity for grace. That's the opportunity for the glory of Resurrection, isn't it?

"I think back to the prayer of Solomon in the Old Testament, and Solomon prayed, 'When your people have sinned, and then they pray and confess your name and turn from their sin, because you punish them, then hear in heaven and forgive the sin of your servants, your people Israel, teach them the good way in which they should walk.'

"So this was the night of breaking the old way of being bishop. I realized that had to end. The old way of being the church in Louisiana, as far as I could see, wouldn't work. I didn't know what would work, but I knew we shared that common fate. All of us were now tied to giving ourselves to that fate.

"The next question was what would we give."

## CHAPTER 6

# MOVIEMAKING
# IN RED STICK

MY FIRST TEN DAYS IN LOUISIANA ARE FRANTIC. I DROP DOWN INTO Baton Rouge (literally translated "Red Stick"), a city whose population has doubled overnight. I have never made a film before. I don't have time to do this in stages. We must simply head out, film interviews, and then figure out what the shape of the narrative will be. Thank God, once again, for friendships forged in seminary. The two priests who lead me to the people I need to meet are both General Seminary graduates. One is now the dean of the cathedral in New Orleans, David Duplantier. The other is Tommy Dillon, rector of St. Augustine's in Baton Rouge.

Tommy introduces me to the Reverend Mary Moody, a ninety-year-old African Methodist Episcopal pastor who takes me under her wing sight unseen and leads me into the world of the black faith community on the north side of Baton Rouge. David connects me with one of the great music icons of New Orleans, Irvin Mayfield, founder and director of the New Orleans Jazz Orchestra.

David is the one who tells me about Irvin's desire to compose a great jazz symphony in tribute to all who have drowned. Irvin's own father is missing, and no one knows if he has survived. I ask, "Is Irvin here?

Could we interview him now?" Within minutes Mayfield and his pianist, Ron Markham, have arrived. We set up to record his performance of *Just a Closer Walk With Thee* in the chapel of St. James.

I am immediately drawn to Irvin as he begins to talk about blues and jazz. He is describing in musical terms all that I have come to believe about metabolizing suffering, watching it transformed into grace. I am bowled over to be in the presence of someone who is not only clearly a creative genius, but also a person of great spiritual depth. As I listen I know Irvin is giving me the soul of the story.

He begins, "Jazz has this great element called blues in it. Blues is to jazz like blood is to the body. I don't mean a genre. What I am talking about is a sound that came from the spirituals, came from the field songs—that thing that Ray Charles put on *America the Beautiful*. Blues says things are bad, but it's gonna be alright.

"Then what jazz says is we can *make* it better, right here, right now with what's available to us. That's what it means to improvise. We can't just take anything if we're going to improve the blues. The key is style and class. You know, like Louis Armstrong did—swing with it. And that's what makes America great. That's what New Orleans and jazz is all about. Dealing with tragedy with style and class to make it better. That's how I know the people of New Orleans are going to turn this into something really, really good."

Then as if to illustrate all that he's just said, Irvin picks up his trumpet and begins to play a jazz funeral version of *A Closer Walk With Thee*. He begins with the first line, the dirge that is played on the way to the grave, and ends with the second line, the upbeat jazzy celebration of the Resurrection that's played after the body's interment.

In the sounds of Irvin's trumpet I can hear the lament of the old spirituals and the jazzy refrains of improvisation and hope. In his music he is telling me a story of the frustrations and aspirations of a battered group of survivors under siege who are greatly in need of divine and human assistance.

I can hear their moans in the bended, bluesy notes of his horn—the dread and despair of unspeakable loss and pain, but the rhythmic facility of the Holy Spirit too. I can hear the deep understanding that intense suffering can yield transcendence and saving grace. That God takes suffering and makes it a stepping-stone for his own liberating power. Takes what we got and makes it better. As I listen I begin to feel what it is to heal from the blues, the healing transforming power of the blues. And I begin to see where we, as persons of faith, must stand in the wake of Hurricane Katrina.

The next day Tommy Dillon puts me in touch with Mary Moody. She asks us to pick her up at her apartment and says she will take us to visit a number of black congregations who have all opened their doors as shelters to folks displaced by the flood. As she comes to the car I can tell from a distance this is no ordinary woman. Although she is ninety, she is lean, straight, and noble—over six feet tall. She is swathed in a floor-length dashiki and crowned with a halo of snow-white hair. Her manner is enormously gracious. I am not surprised as we begin to enter churches that the sight of her brings crowds. I think to myself, "This must be just a little like what it was to travel with Jesus. People flocking to be near his aura of holiness—literally reaching out to touch the hem of his garment." That is the type of reception Mary Moody receives everywhere she goes.

She is an incredible extemporaneous preacher. The minute we turn on the camera at our first stop, Greater Green Chapel AME, she preaches the words that will frame all my scenes of people serving one another throughout the city of Baton Rouge.

"All power rests in his hands. God is all-powerful. And I'm just so grateful we are touching lives. You know he claims—yes he gets our attention. And sometimes we think we can get past him. But the joy in life is knowing who he is. And he said, 'Feed the hungry. Visit the sick. Visit those who are in prison.' But he said something else. 'In as much as you have done it unto the least of these my brethren you have done it unto me.' So when we touch our fellow man it makes a difference, because as we touch him, and touch her, and touch them, we are touching Christ. And he wants us to love ye one another. But he didn't leave it to chance. No, he didn't leave it to chance. He said, 'As I have loved you.'"

After Mary speaks there is that thick, hushed presence in the room that reminds me of the chapel at Ground Zero. I look across at my twenty-one-year-old brother, Simon, who is not particularly religious but cares about justice deeply. Big tears are rolling down his face. The other five or six AME pastors clustered behind Mary are saying, "Amen, sister." "Preach it." One pastor standing directly behind Mary has on a black t-shirt with big white letters on it saying, "Got Jesus?" Clearly Mother Mary does.

Other pastors begin to speak. "Our people, some of them are hurt because it took a long time for government to respond. Trucks passed them by and would not help them." Leroy Brown, a former player for the Chicago Bears and now an AME pastor in New Orleans, asks, "Have you ever lost everything? I lost everything." He has nothing but the blessed news, after a week of not knowing, that his daughter is alive. Still he exclaims, "But my spirit's still high. I know there is a God! God did not bring me this far to leave me." Leroy's voice rises further. "The most important thing I want to do is go back to New Orleans to knock on some doors because there are three or four thousand people still inside of some houses that cannot be gotten out. The city needs us to knock down some doors and bring 'em out. See whose parents that is, whose son that is, whose daughter that is. Because they are somebody's people! I need to get down there. I'm cryin' to get down there!"

I am amazed to discover only a few hours later that is exactly what battalions of good ol' boys with boats are out there doing. At the airport I interview men and their sons who have taken their boats to rescue people trapped in their attics. The fathers drive the boats, while their sons climb up on the roofs and bang on them. Then they listen closely to hear if someone pounds back in response. If they hear someone they start to hack at the roof until they open up a hole large enough for someone to climb out. Often they encounter the drowned corpses of family members floating in attics next to one who survived.

Riding around the city with Mary and talking about this huge biracial outpouring, she says she is reminded of a song the children of Fiji taught her when she visited there. The words she recites become my Louisiana mantra: "Bind us together, Lord. Bind us together. Bind us with cords that cannot be broken. Bind us together, Lord. Bind us together with love."

As we film the woman organizing the cooking of all the food at the downtown convention center, I meet the church volunteers from not only the Episcopal, but the Presbyterian, Methodist, and Baptist churches downtown, sheltering and feeding mothers evacuated from New Orleans hospitals with their newborn babies, and find out the women and children were in fact rescued from the hospital by escaped prisoners. As I tour Sister Irma Miller's "Love Center" shelter at Mt. Pilgrim Baptist Church, "Where Everybody is Somebody and Jesus

Christ is Lord," and read their marquee that proclaims, "This Church Is Prayer Conditioned," it is clear that a new kind of bonding is indeed taking place across the Baton Rouge community.

Working on the script to accompany all these scenes, I am moved to return to the metaphor of New Orleans's musical heritage. I pull out my Wynton Marsalis CD of Stanley Crouch's "Premature Autopsies," and my *Cornell West Reader* to hunker down and think.

New Orleans was, and hopefully will be again, a multicultural city invigorated by what Stanley Crouch calls "the refined and impassioned depiction of the power, and the presence and the possibility of the human spirit." That is what jazz is about—that human spirit's power and possibility. I am just beginning to realize that jazz is the sound of the brave, devoted, noble human spirit declaring against all odds, all failings, all separation, all hatred, all hurt that we were made for one another. Declaring that the human spirit was made to forge one diverse and syncopated body.

So I wonder as I travel the streets of Baton Rouge in the week following Katrina, "Is this our core belief in white America? Or do we still need help from our brothers and sisters of color to understand the unfulfilled imperative this music seeks to communicate?" We say we love the music of New Orleans but do we get what its message is really about?

I think about the experience of elation we felt at Ground Zero when we began to live without division, helping one another with open hearts. This fuses with the images and the metaphors that surround me in Baton Rouge, as I pen the closing words of the film's script.

In my mind the torch from the Little Chapel and the message carried in the spiritual blues impulse are virtually the same. What if the church claimed this vision, to forge this kind of mutual availability and gratitude across the races as our goal in the recovery from Katrina? I have the sense that we would create a kind of growing, soaring sound—yet another verse in the song of an American awakening.

Then the beat of our essence will surely swing with the beauty
   of living.
The trumpet of our soul will sound with the glory of life.
The drum of our heart will pound with the confirmation of
   our connection.
And we will feel the emotional magnificence of life.
The joy of being human and living that love for real.

Could it be that after Katrina we are ready to imagine the glory of God's whole Rebirth Brass Band swinging low, swinging high in a rhythm that might just change everything? Mary Moody does more than hope. It's as if she can already see it. Before I leave for the airport she tells me, "Go to the book of Isaiah, the forty-third chapter, verses eighteen and nineteen. 'Do not remember the former things, nor consider the things of old. Behold, in spite of all this, behold, I will do a new thing. It shall spring forth. Shall ye not know it? I will put a road in the wilderness and rivers in the desert.' Now, Courtney," Mary says, "Baby, that's new. Totally new."

## CHAPTER 7

# THE JERICHO ROAD

FROM BATON ROUGE I TRAVEL TO ATLANTA TO WORK WITH THE MEDIA Center on finishing the film. The following week I am back in New York City. No sooner do I unlock the door to my apartment than the telephone rings. It is Abagail Nelson, vice president of Episcopal Relief and Development and most recently my roommate in Louisiana. She goes straight to the point. "Courtney, the woman we hired to set up the Office of Disaster Response for the bishop has resigned. We're looking for her replacement. Would you consider becoming the director of the Office of Disaster Response for the Diocese of Louisiana?"

I am a complete novice when it comes to working in low-income neighborhoods. Abagail, with her master's from the London School of Economics and years of experience working in challenged communities around the world, knows far more about this than do I. But after a few weeks of back and forth, Abagail and I settle on an agreement. Soon I'm involved in meetings and conference calls weekly as we plan for a December roll out of the work to be funded by a $3.2 million ERD grant—the largest for domestic disaster recovery in the history of the Episcopal Church. It's daunting.

Bit by bit I learn. A decisive moment comes at a meeting in early November with the Louisiana diocese's canon for mission, Chad Jones, and a potential partner we are meeting named Ruama Camp. Both have flown to New York to discuss the possibility of contracting with Ruama's nonprofit, Grace Community Services, to run a case management program working with Katrina survivors.

Ruama tells us stories she has heard as she worked with some of our displaced survivors in Houston. The most shocking is one of a young mother who was encamped in the Superdome. Her baby died while they were waiting for help to come, and the mother had no option of what to do with her baby's body, but to put it in an ice chest that still had a little bit of ice in it. When the buses finally came the Guards would not allow her to take the cooler with her on the bus. The mother was horribly traumatized—almost catatonic by the time Ruama met her in Houston.

Then Ru says to us, "This is the situation. We have tens of thousands of people who are in desperate straits. The public has no idea what their story really is and probably never will. Because the people I am talking about have no voice." She mouths the words, "Help me! Help me!" but no sound escapes her lips.

"That's what it's like," she explains. "Tens of thousands of people screaming "Help me!" but we do not hear them. They are in pain. They are in need. They are the ones who can tell us what we can do to help them. But they are scattered across 18,000 U.S. zip codes, and no one can hear their pleas. They have no voice."

Immediately, a person's face pops into my mind. It is the face of Carolyn Lukensmeyer, a woman I came to know the summer after 9/11. Carolyn is the founder and director of a nonprofit in Washington, D.C. named America*Speaks*.

In the summer of 2002, her firm conducted a five-thousand-person electronic town hall meeting at the Jacob Javits Center in New York that lasted all day to discuss the first round of proposed plans for the 9/11 memorial and the redevelopment of Lower Manhattan. A large number of members of the chapel community participated in the gathering, called Listening to the City, and found it to be a thrilling experience: thousands of fellow New Yorkers, being citizens together, feeling the dignity of that as we participated in a fascinating and artfully facilitated deliberation and decision-making process.

The first assignment Bishop Jenkins gives me is to reach out to my old boss Jamie Callaway at Trinity Grants. Very quickly Jamie suggests that we plan a visioning retreat for the bishop at Trinity in New York. He provides conference facilities in Trinity's office tower to gather experts for a two-day discussion. Carolyn Lukensmeyer will be one of the speaker participants, and Ruama Camp will be there too.

On the second day of our meeting Carolyn takes the floor last. She begins by stating that she has been crushed by our country's recent experience in New Orleans—the spectacle of the outrages to human beings we witnessed after the storm. She states very clearly that in her opinion our federal government let New Orleans down. Prior to Katrina many in our country believed that issues of race and class in our nation were really not that bad. Very few people were still locked into structures that trapped them in poverty. That was the general wisdom.

But, Carolyn continues, what the nation saw in New Orleans lifted the veil on poverty in America and dramatized the heartbreaking disparity that still exists. Carolyn movingly recalls one moment in particular when an elderly African American woman was filmed sobbing, shaking her head, saying over and over in disbelief of her plight, "But I am an American. I am an American. How can this happen in America?" It is the same image that brought the bishop to his knees.

Then Carolyn frames the essential question as she sees it. "We are at a crossroads in the course of American democracy. There has always been a gap between the aspiration of our country's ideals and the reality. But now we have seen a dramatization of that gap between aspiration and reality that morally cannot be ignored. This is beyond simply race and class. This is about American morality. The moral response we choose to make in this recovery will tell us whether we are going to be the country we say we are or not.

"We cannot avoid this question. We are going to make a collective choice. Either we are or we aren't America. This is a defining moment that will declare who we are as a nation.

"Every single one of us will make that choice. Every person in a role of institutional leadership will make that choice. Yes or no. We will either seize the opportunity, make the moral choice and advance democracy or we will shun our moral responsibility as American citizens and set ourselves back as a society for decades to come."

By the end of her heartfelt testimonial the whole room is collectively grave. Bishop Jenkins looks like a deer in the headlights. I ask him quietly what he thinks and he says, "She scared me to death. I'm terrified. I see what is at stake and the responsibility, on a level I never recognized before."

When we have the chance for the bishop to explain to me more fully what he meant, Charles Jenkins says, "I was fortunately standing next to a column, because when Carolyn spoke I needed support. I actually had to rest my back against the support of that column when she said, 'This is not about you.' That is what I heard her say. 'This is not about you, or not wholly about you. This is about the nation.' When she said, 'New Orleans is an American opportunity,' it was like somebody hit me with a whole entire bottle of Aqua Velva aftershave. Do you remember that commercial? Whack!' That pushed me back against the column. The physicalness of it. I was thinking, 'This is not about you, Charles. It's not about the people of New Orleans.' And what a tremendous relief that is when you depersonalize. 'It's not about me.' But at the same time what a huge responsibility it is when you realize, 'It's about us. It's about all of us.'

"And at that point, the morning that Carolyn opened my eyes so much, the twenty-first chapter of the Revelation of St. John came. It was put in front of me, and it came to have new meaning in that moment. 'I saw a new heaven and a new earth; for the first heaven and the first earth had passed away . . . the holy city, the new Jerusalem, coming down out of heaven from God. . . . And I heard a loud voice from the throne saying, 'See the home of God is among mortals. . . . Mourning and crying and pain will be no more for the first things have passed away. . . . See I am making all things new.' And I saw that of course this would be part of the struggle because the first things are so attractive to some. And I knew we would have to try to articulate the new things of the kingdom of God that are immensely more attractive. The things that we are free to be."

In New York the next morning, a group of Louisiana clergy, the bishop, and I convene to discuss all that we have heard in our meetings and reach a consensus on what we believe the mission of the Office of Disaster Response ought to be. We will give ourselves to bringing people home with dignity and help build a stronger future by creating opportunities for youth. To create solutions we will support citizen engagement that particularly strives for a representative majority of low-income members of the community.

The week following the meeting in New York is the week commemorating the birthday of Martin Luther King Jr. We return to New Orleans for the first full meeting of the pre- and post-Katrina diocesan staff. There are about a dozen extremely loyal, longtime employees and then there are all of us newcomers.

Jenkins comes into the office with no idea what he is going to say to us. He is praying for God to guide him. He decides to go to Dr. King for inspiration. As the bishop is flipping through the pages of a collection of King's writings, he remembers the speech preached from Riverside Church in New York in April 1967, "Beyond Vietnam." He remembers it because of the impact the broadcast of the speech had in the living room of his family's home when he heard it as a youngster.

"So there I was in Desoto Parish Louisiana. I was raised in a household where my parents were receptive to Dr. King. I can remember making a racist comment as a child and being punished by my parents—being severely punished. We were watching King's speech that night with Uncle Walter Cronkite on the CBS news, asking, "What is this all about?" Even though my father admired King he could not understand the connection that Dr. King was making between the morality of the civil rights movement in the United States and the Vietnam War. The speech was a challenge that hit my family hard."

The memories draw the bishop to reread the speech on this morning of Martin Luther King Day, January 2006, thirty-nine years later. As he is reading, a passage jumps off the page. It is the passage about the Jericho Road.

The staff meeting is called to order by the bishop, who begins by saying to all of us, "My vision has been raised so high from my time in New York that I feel like I'm walkin' around lookin' at the sky." He says that he believes the church is being called to a new mission that all of us who work on this team will play important roles in implementing.

Then the bishop opens his Bible, and in his low, soft northern Louisiana drawl he begins to read from the gospel of Luke.

> A man was going down from Jerusalem to Jericho, and fell into the hands of robbers, who stripped him, beat him, and went away, leaving him half dead. Now by chance a priest was going down that road; and when he saw him, he passed on the other side. So likewise a Levite, when he came to the place and saw him, passed by on the other side. But a Samaritan while traveling came near him; and when he saw him, he was moved with pity. He went to him and bandaged his wounds, having poured oil and wine on them. Then he put him on his own animal, brought him to an inn, and took care of him. The next

day he took out two denarii, gave them to the innkeeper, and said, "Take care of him; and when I come back, I will repay you whatever more you spend." "Which of these three, do you think, was a neighbor to the man who fell into the hands of robbers?" He [the disciple] said, "The one who showed him mercy." Jesus said to him, "Go and do likewise."

Then Jenkins closes his Bible and opens the collection of speeches by Dr. King. Without speaking or commenting, the bishop continues to read in the same voice.

A true revolution of values will soon cause us to question the fairness and justice of many of our past and present policies. On the one hand we are called to play the Good Samaritan on life's roadside; but that will be only an initial act. One day we must come to see that the whole Jericho road must be transformed so that men and women will not be constantly beaten and robbed as they make their journey on life's highway. True compassion is more than flinging a coin to a beggar; it is not haphazard and superficial. It comes to see that an edifice which produces beggars needs restructuring. A true revolution of values will soon look uneasily on the glaring contrast of poverty and wealth.

This choice by Bishop Jenkins, to go to the text of this particular speech and to discover there the words that will guide him and all of us through our work says volumes to me about who Charles Jenkins is. On the outside Jenkins is the quintessential Louisiana country boy—hearty, congenial, full of earthy humor. I know he has been reared in one of the most conservative regions of the Deep South on his family's cotton farm. He is an alumnus of one of the most traditionalist seminaries in our church. He is a Republican and knows the elder George H. W. Bush.

I wonder if he has been studying King's speech, because the thrust of the speech as a whole, in addition to the passage the bishop chooses to read to us, is precisely about the choice and the question Carolyn has posed.

In its entirety "Beyond Vietnam" is a speech about the spiritual health of America in a time of war. King addresses directly what the question of the morality of the war has to do with his commitment to civil rights and the eradication of poverty. He says that the country was on a path of "real promise and hope for the poor—black and white—

through the poverty program" he and many others had sacrificed and fought so hard to implement in the early 1960s. And then came the war that began "to drain men and skills and money like some demonic destructive suction tube." So King describes how war is an enemy to the poor because of the way it diverts our country's resources away from empowering life, liberty, and happiness for all our people.

"Beyond Vietnam" is a deeply patriotic speech. King frames his whole life's work as deriving from a "concern for the integrity and life of America." He says that all those who have been drawn to the movement "are working for the health of our land." He reminds the gathered crowd that the motto of the Southern Christian Leadership Council (founded in New Orleans) is "To Save the Soul of America." Quite simply, King says that America cannot be saved "as long as it destroys the deepest hopes of people."

I come away from the meeting impressed that the bishop has found the speech by King that fits our time and our moral challenge so perfectly, and that he is clearly thinking and praying over these issues. It is a while before I get to hear what was going through his head.

When the passage leapt off the page and grabbed his attention, it was a moment of liberation. Jenkins was worried about what the main thrust of the response of the Episcopal Church would be in the long term. He felt before New York, in the months from September through December, that "we were making some good beginnings, but our path wasn't obvious. We didn't have huge trucks with a thousand pounds of salvific ice on 'em. I was watching that first response by other churches, and here I am thinking, 'You just don't have what you would need to do that.' We could not follow in that model. And then we went to New York, and the first morning back Dr. King gave me permission not to have to follow that more obvious, conventional model, but to see that there is a longer model, and that was the road for us."

"The Samaritan provided for the man whose life was thrown in the ditch. The Samaritan did that. Then Dr. King says, 'Alright *we* have got to transform the Jericho Road.' So that was a great moment of freedom for me to come upon, to be guided to that passage. It was through Dr. King's words that I finally could hear it—that we have a longer-term response. And that response is the transformation of the Jericho Road.

"As Dr. King said, 'You've got to realize when people have been beaten and robbed of the things of life and dignity, and left to die in the ditch—we've got to do something about *that road*.' I came in that

Monday morning and I was praying for the Lord to show me something. That's where I went."

We begin the work to persuade the powers-that-be to bring America*Speaks* to conduct a multi-city electronic townhall format for New Orleans' city-wide planning process. These efforts bring me into the orbit of every person who will become a part of the uncommon team we forge. I meet Nell Bolton who, I learn, has arrived from Africa and is serving as minister for social renewal at Trinity. I meet Gus Newport, Shakoor Aljuwani, and Mary Fontenot—three African American leaders who will become treasured mentors. They are the ones who begin to paint the picture I need to grasp.

A paper has been published by a civil rights attorney in town named Bill Quigley entitled, "Six Months After Katrina—Who Was Left Behind? Then and Now." Quigley has done the analysis. Of the 270,000 evacuees who began their post-Katrina odyssey in shelters, 93 percent are African American, 68 percent neither had money in the bank nor a usable credit card; 55 percent do not have a car and 64 percent were renters; 22 percent stayed behind because they were caring for someone who was physically unable to leave; and 76 percent have children under the age of eighteen years old with them. The population of the damaged areas of the city was 45.8 percent African American, 45.7 percent living in rental housing, and 20.9 percent living below the poverty line.

But of the $6.2 billion in Community Development Block Grant funding only $1 billion, according to the governor, could be used to encourage the rebuilding of affordable housing. So, Quigley points out, with 45 percent of the damaged homes occupied by renters, affordable housing "could" end up with 16 percent of the assistance. There is a 78 percent reduction in the number of hospitals, and most of the public schools have either not reopened or are being converted into charter schools with selective admissions policies.

Even the secretary of Housing and Urban Development, Alphonso Jackson, has been quoted as telling a Houston audience, "New Orleans is not going to be as black as it was for a long time, if ever again." Quigley concludes that the city is "at risk of losing 80 percent of its black population."

This situation sounds to me, and to many gathered in the room at our first convening of organizers from across the city, like a formula for once again devastating the deepest hopes and aspirations of a huge segment of our community who longs to come home and contribute to the rebuilding and re-creation of the city. But if we can ensure that everyone contributes, everyone is included, everyone is re-gathered to participate in setting the city's rebuilding agenda, maybe we really can begin to change the Jericho Road.

There is no particular reason either Shakoor, a former Black Panther, or Gus, former mayor of Berkeley, California, and a one-time protégé of Malcolm X, should decide to reach out to us, the Episcopal Church, but within weeks we are beginning to make friends with one another. Shakoor takes a group of our Office of Disaster Response staff, working with volunteers to build Homecoming Centers, on an all-day tour of the work that Malik's group, Common Ground, is doing. It is in the course of this tour that the leadership of youth from every corner of this nation begins to emerge in my mind as one of the greatest signs of hope for the future.

Shakoor tells us about the genesis of Common Ground as we drive the Ninth Ward. "We was telling thousands there is no power and no lights and you will be in an area where most folks would fear to tread—one of the most dangerous neighborhoods in New Orleans before the storm. But you couldn't stop people from coming. College students especially were willing to risk everything to help people they didn't even know, and for most of these students, helping people who were completely opposite of those they'd grown up with or were accustomed to.

"I'd seen this kind of thing, but never on this kind of scale. Now I'm supervising a thousand volunteers a day. The enormity of it—that is the thing for me. Before this I had thought this country would inch along. In fact I was at the point in my life where I thought I would never really see massive change in this country. I figured the way things were—we were kind of in a deep slumber and given my life span—I only had another ten maybe twenty years tops—that I might not see much in the way of change given how uncertain things had gotten.

"And then all these young people—that changed it for me. It reawakened something that I kind of knew—that things can change overnight. When you cannot see it, something else is there dwelling, invisible but gathering strength and rising up. And as I've worked with Common Ground I've begun to think maybe there is enough basic goodness to change the direction of this country, and maybe in the not-too-distant future. I began to see maybe something new was coming. And maybe I'd get to be in the mix and see it before I died.

"It started with a small group of students but it has grown to be a broad college network of over two hundred colleges. It is growing because when the students go back they hold meetings, and show slide shows of their time. And now it is just snowballing from a group of fifteen to twenty, then fifty colleges, then a hundred and so on.

"Just seeing that kind of people power—seeing students from around the country and residents of the Ninth Ward, and parents and teachers—standing up. It is giving me hope. You wait for the right time to take that kind of leap of faith. Now I know New Orleans is one of those times. I've worked my whole life long for this."

In turn we show Shakoor our gutting operation. An outstanding volunteer, recently graduated from Grinnell University in Iowa, Katie Mears, who heads the program, is one of those recent college grads giving us all hope. Katie and team member Holly Heine are recruiting thousands of Episcopalian volunteers also flocking to the side of their neighbors in the drastically broken landscape that is New Orleans.

Katie is working with college volunteers and often with prosperous white Episcopalians. Most are seeing how low-income people live for the first time in our lives and the experience is forming a strong commitment to achieving greater equity in America. Katie hears from students and young professionals alike how difficult it is to go back to their former lives after drawing close to such suffering and pain. Feeling that they have really helped somebody here, volunteers are often reluctant to return to desk jobs and lives they feel are pretty meaningless. They want to come back. The word is spreading through our youth and church members from around the nation in the same self-organized, peer-to-peer fashion Shakoor is seeing from his sightline with Common Ground.

Katie's teams work everywhere in the city. Many homeowners are just traveling back to New Orleans, driving up to their house for the first time months after the storm. Doing that takes enormous emotional energy and courage. Then they walk in the door and collapse. They look and the wreckage and think, "I can't do this." So for a team of strangers to say, "It's okay. Don't worry. We'll do this part for you," is an enormous gift. The gratitude that families feel is beyond words.

Katie decides that our church is going to make people with special challenges our priority. "People who are dying. People so depressed they cannot talk. They are our people." Her philosophy is simple: "Certain people in this community understand that many with power and resources have given up on their recovery. Giving up on anyone seems absolutely ridiculous to me."

In the summer of 2006, Shakoor Aljuwani begins to talk to Gus Newport about the fact that much to his surprise, of all the groups he is coming to know in New Orleans, the Episcopal Church seems the most sincerely committed to resident-led redevelopment. Gus, Shakoor, and I all pile in the car with former public attorney Brad Powers, who is the head of our new affordable housing development corporation, Jericho Road.

We begin to drive up and down the streets of severely blighted Central City—the neighborhood where I first learn of an outstanding grassroots leader named Saundra Reed. All the while Gus (also former Executive Director of the Dudley Street Neighborhood Initiative in Roxbury, Massachusetts) gives a running commentary and analysis of what it will take to really involve and engage the residents of the neighborhood in taking control and turning their community around.

Then one day Gus calls with a surprising question that catches me off guard. "Would the Episcopal Church have any interest in hiring Shakoor to be a community organizer?" It is an idea, though surprising, that intrigues me. There are so many different areas of our work that would greatly benefit from Shakoor's expertise.

Unfortunately, I have a little money in the budget I could spend on this, but not enough. Immediately Mary Fontenot, lead organizer of All Congregations Together (ACT), leaps to mind. What if, I think, we jointly hired Shakoor, and the diocese joined with All Congregations Together in supporting Shakoor to work for us both?

In a matter of weeks, months of work pays off, and we forge an agreement with Fontenot to jointly hire Shakoor. The diocese opens a Homecoming Center at a historic black church named St. Luke's, and America*Speaks* signs a memorandum of agreement to implement a multi-city, satellite-linked process. I am learning this is the way things happen in the recovery of New Orleans. Everything seems to take forever. Then everything gels at once. My first six-month commitment has come and gone, my second six-month commitment is almost over, but we are finally beginning to see real progress.

The pace is hard to one used to the New York minute. If not for Mark Stevenson, canon for administration for the diocese, I might not still be hanging in. It was Mark who encouraged me, when I was at my wits' end and at a crucial juncture of choosing whether to stay or go,

"Remember what Mother Teresa said. 'We are not called to be successful. We are called to be faithful.'"

I draw on those words and I draw on the spiritual refreshment and nourishment I am finding at St. Luke's, where we are about to open the first Homecoming Center in the city. Nearly every member of the congregation, the majority of whom lived in the reclaimed swampland of New Orleans East, lost everything they had at the time of the storm. The church, in Treme, one of New Orleans's most historic Creole neighborhoods, took several feet of water and had to be reclaimed from scratch. But the people of St. Luke's, although they were scattered far and wide, decide, after the storm when their lives are in tatters, that their first priority, with whatever resources can be mustered, is to rebuild and restore their spiritual home, even before they turn to the work of restoring their personal homes.

The congregation greets me warmly. The worship is incredible. At many points I am overwhelmed by feeling the fervent faith of persons who are suffering so much. It is especially powerful when the entire congregation, whose numbers are beginning to swell with helpers coming from everywhere in the country, joins hands and sings together the "Our Father." At the point when we belt out, "For Thine is the Kingdom, and the Power, and the Glory, Forever!" everyone lifts their clasped hands to the sky. After church Shakoor says, "There was so much Spirit in that room I thought the roof of the church was going to blow right off."

Now we decide to fuse organizing for the Community Congress with our first efforts at outreach in the community surrounding St. Luke's. Shakoor, Ellene Stampley, our Homecoming Center coordinator, a positive rapper named Joe Blakk, and I are working furiously to register as many people for the electronic town hall Community Congress as possible. On the sign-up sheets are spaces to record ethnicity, gender, income, and age, as the goal is to have a body in the room with the precise demographics of the city as a whole pre-Katrina. Similar teams to ours in New Orleans are doing this in Texas, northern Louisiana, and Georgia.

The day of the citywide meeting to set the recovery plan for the city arrives, and the location, as I dreamed, is at the Morial Convention Center, the site where the haunting image of the elderly African American woman with the sign, "I am an American Too," was filmed. We will be working in an enormous room with hundreds and hundreds of round tables filling the space. Massive flat screens to link us with thousands more missing neighbors in four other diaspora cities make for a dramatic visual effect.

Nell is working as a facilitator and has been instrumental in organizing this aspect of the event. Shakoor and I are being trained to be part of something called the "Theme Team." Our job, along with about thirty other people, is to read all the verbatim conversations coming in from all the tables in all the rooms in every city and to look for common themes.

On the morning of the event Carolyn takes the podium. She speaks from a deep place that really gathers the room. "No one who was not in New Orleans at the time of Katrina and did not experience the storm directly can ever really know what that was like, what really happened to those of you who lived through it."

The big flat screen TVs are showing the faces of thousands people still living in exile. I am praying Mary Moody's mantra, "bind us together Lord, bind us together," as Carolyn begins. "Every human being needs to know they are loved and their voice will be heard. That is why we are here today. I know that many have been through a year that makes it very difficult to trust any public process. But I am asking for your trust for the sake of this city. To make this conversation what it has the potential to be, we need to speak to one another today from a place of trust. And I am asking you to make the deeper choice."

And so we begin. I keep thinking of Ruama, and the conversation a year before about the fact that no one would ever hear the voice of the survivors we watched on our TVs. But here we are, building a new city and new society, a society of shared fate and common values and hopes and dreams together. This is the power of democratic citizenship and of faith at its best.

Carolyn remembers, "Tons of people came up to me afterwards and said, 'This is the first time the city has felt whole since Katrina,' and it gives me chills even to think about what a powerful experience it was. People re-owned the city, and people who had been separated from their home and separated from their people, could see each other and talk to each other, and everyone knew they were all having the same unifying, healing, and hopeful experience. Nobody really believed people would come to a clear agreement but they did."

The theme of youth and education rises to the fore. After flood protection, the highest priority for investment is better schools, with better-paid teachers and improved administrations. Residents want planners to make schools the central focus of rebuilding designs, and to plan neighborhoods around these 24/7, community-centered, educational institutions. Next, government is directed to invest in healthcare. Finally, a clear mandate is given with regard to developing low-income and affordable housing. Residents want government and planning experts to tackle poverty, not through "social re-engineering" of low-income people from the city, but by creating homeownership for low-income and public housing residents.

Afterwards there's a little party to celebrate. Carey Shea from the Rockefeller Foundation, instrumental in turning the corner on hiring America *Speaks*, gives me a thumbs-up from across the room. Carolyn hugs me, laughing and crying at the same time as we recall all the crazy rollercoaster moments. Gus Newport says with a big smile, "Well, Dr. Cowart, I think I owe you a drink."

The bishop remembers with a wry smile that we were warned by some in the city not to get involved in doing this. "And now we've moved from a first meeting and demographic of two hundred people from one neighborhood in New Orleans, to a demographic that is finally representative. I was hearing real concern from people who were saying, 'Don't do it, Charles, because you are only going to hurt people and disappoint them. Leave 'em alone.'

"But we've come together as a *civitas* and we've worked responsibly together. We heard a lot of different voices. We honored the dignity of one another in a demographic that truly represented our city pre-Katrina in almost every way except age. We took a risk.

"It was a truly wonderful picture of what the city can be. We can sit down and engage in responsible discourse. We can move beyond self-interest toward the interest of 'we.' As Rabbi Sachs says, 'The many 'I's' can become 'we,' and that doesn't mean 'I' ceases to exist. I think this city is ready to be involved in that kind of covenant relationship.

"Sachs says there are three ways to get people to do things. You can pay them, and that's the way of the market. You can force them, and that's the way of power. And third, you can go into covenant where it's not so important that you get what you want, but that everybody gives. And today there was giving. *Everyone* was giving. That is how we build the New Jerusalem. That is how we change the Jericho Road."

## CHAPTER 8

# WHOSE HOOD IS THE HARDEST?

NO ONE EXPECTS THE MESSAGE DELIVERED BY THE TALL, SMILING, affable young man named Donald Jackson who has come to address our first community dinner at St. Luke's. He begins pleasantly enough, by saying how grateful he is to St. Luke's for giving him an opportunity to talk about the school where he is serving as principal next door. Jackson receives a round of applause when he acknowledges that our site coordinator's mom, Mrs. Stampley, was the teacher who inspired him to want to be a teacher himself.

Then the engaging smile disappears from Mr. Jackson's face. Before the storm John Mac, as everyone calls his high school, was considered the lowest ranked public high school in America. Louisiana was ranked last in the nation. New Orleans Parish was ranked last in Louisiana. And John Mac was ranked last in New Orleans.

"It was bad then," Jackson tells us, "but it is worse now. We have eight hundred students attending, fifteen teachers, and twenty-six security guards." This time the principal's revelation is followed, not by applause, but by a collective gasp of shock. Jackson continues, "Forty percent of our students are back in the city without either parent. They are squatting in gutted houses, living with boyfriends, sleeping on different sofas night to night. And when they come to school we have no textbooks, not one book in our library, no doors on the bathroom stalls, frozen-solid meals are handed out at lunchtime. We have no Internet connection for the few computer monitors, and as you realize from the numbers I gave you, we have anywhere from forty to sixty students in a classroom."

When we turn to a community discussion of what the Homecoming Center's focus should be, the decision is unanimous. Church members and neighbors alike want to focus entirely on supporting John Mac. It feels amazing to have found a clear direction so quickly. We make an appointment to meet with Jackson the following week.

I've never been inside a school like John McDonough. On the outside it is a huge red brick fortress with metal screens on all the windows. On the inside it is like a prison. In the morning there are hundreds of teenagers congregated outside in their chosen uniform of black baggy pants and huge oversize white t-shirts. When it is time for class to begin, NOPD cops in police cars literally herd the young people into the building by driving their police cars up on the sidewalk, blue lights flashing. It all seems incredibly degrading to me.

When you enter the building you must first pass through a metal detector that screens for guns and knives. There are security guards in blue uniforms everywhere. The building looks like it hasn't been painted in years. I think to myself, "Is this any kind of environment for learning?" Jackson takes us on a tour. Sure enough the library has lots of gray metal bookcases but there isn't a single book on any of them. The bathrooms also prove to be true to his description. Not only are there no doors on the stalls, there aren't even knobs to turn the water spigots on the sinks.

Shakoor and Ellene begin to visit the school almost daily. Shakoor remembers, "It was chaotic—way too many kids. The classrooms were dreary. Teachers were trying to make it work, trying to keep order. But what do you do in a situation like that? All you can do is try to keep chaos from ensuing, and depending on the teacher, some were able to do that but a lot of them weren't.

"Obviously no one should be called upon to do that, particularly when this was not just forty to sixty ordinary kids in a room. These were kids, many of whom had sat on rooftops for days, had been separated from their families, sent to different states, and were just returning to New Orleans to what? So these were traumatized kids.

"In any other system, under much less stressful conditions, they would have been receiving all types of special care. It was like being in some kind of triage unit, with principals, and administrators, and police and guards running from one point to the next."

A week after our dinner John Mac makes the front page of the *New York Times*. I can't believe it when I pick up my morning copy of the paper and there is Donald Jackson's photo on the upper fold. It turns out a group of students have staged a walk out from school and marched into the City Council chambers to make their grievances known before the city's education committee.

The teens have named themselves the Fyre Youth Squad. To be "fyre" means to be hot, unstoppable in your passion and determination. The students have made presentations describing the conditions in their school and made ardent pleas to decision-makers that they want a first-class, twenty-first-century education. Shakoor has connected with the squad's mentors, Broderick Webb and Liberty Rashad. It is decided that Fyre Youth will make the Homecoming Center their clubhouse, holding evening planning meetings there two or three times a week.

Our regard for the youth grows every day. Shakoor says, "Throughout that relationship with every encounter—many times tears were brought to my eyes by their courage, their intelligence, their compassion. They could have done like a lot of other kids and just rolled with it, tried to scam it, or run away from it. But they decided they were going to step into the fray and fight."

There's tall, gorgeous India, a brilliant speaker who dreams of studying for a political science degree at Tulane, but she is nearly twenty years old and still trying to finish her senior year. It's hard with a two-year-old child. Shakoor says she has the best political, organizing instincts of any youth leader he has ever met in his career of mentoring literally thousands of youth, but she is about to give up and drop out.

"I think India is one of the most articulate spokespersons I've met in New Orleans, period. I watched her over and over stand up and elegantly argue the case for why there should be a world-class, quality education for her peers and stand up to all types of bureaucrats and administrators and expose their lies, demanding what ought to be a God-given right. It was amazing to me—all this talent and they had no place to meet. I was glad we could offer them a home."

There is towering, gentle Floyd, known in the hood as "2 Tall," who shows his true colors at a meeting one night. The kids are having a planning session in the rectory of St. Luke's. I'm back in the kitchen on my cell. Floyd comes in with two plastic cups in his hands, the lips of the cups pressed together to make a kind of container. He is carrying it with great care, and asks me to open the kitchen door so he can step outside. In a minute he comes back in, "That's better," he says. "I feel much better now."

"What are you up to, Floyd?" I ask. He says, "Well, I was sittin' there in the meetin' and there was a bee down on the floor by my foot. At first I was just going to squash it. And then I thought, 'Naw, that bee deserves a better life than that.'" So he scooped it up in a plastic cup, and covered one cup with another to make a little cage. Then gently carried the bee outside to release it. "And these," I think to myself, "are the kids who are viewed when they walk down the street as a menace to society. It's horrible."

2 Tall is a special education kid with learning disabilities who becomes an outstanding leader. Shakoor underscores that "it was 2 Tall who actually helped force the state to abide by the state laws on special ed through his example, stepping up and testifying before numerous bodies about how special ed students like him were being denied what has become standard in any school in the country for decades." The day we travel to Baton Rouge to support the squad as they testify before BESE, the state Board of Elementary and Secondary Education, there is something about the sight of 2 Tall standing amid the damask-covered antique settees and brocade swags of the governor's mansion parlor, next to the baby grand piano, delivering the speech I have seen him rehearse for ten days in a row, to the governor's chief of staff, that undoes me.

I am so deeply moved by the sheer courage and determination he is exhibiting. Knowing the neglected and decaying surroundings that comprise 2 Tall's world, it seems like a miracle that he is standing here amid the trappings of power and wealth, shining, holding a whole room of people rapt with the power of his simple, innocent, utterly vulnerable honesty.

A teacher at John Mac named Shedrick White expresses what I am feeling in a conversation he and I have one day. "Kids are only a product of something. The rapper Tupac had a book of poetry called *The Rose that Grew from the Concrete*. The concrete represents death. So if you are a rose growin' up from the concrete nobody's gonna criticize and say, 'Well look how it's ruffled up.' Or 'Look how its petals are missin'.' You goin' to be amazed that it even grew from the concrete, from those conditions because it wasn't even supposed to survive.

"And what's makin' the kids so passionate is they had a kind of awakenin' when they were evacuated and got to see what other cities' educational systems look like. So when you talk to the kids they are like, 'Man, we had it made out there. Computers everywhere. I'd have one class in one building, and another class in another building. I was on a *campus*."

By supporting the kids we begin to learn how rough their lives really are. At night we each take a car-full to where they are sleeping, after they've been in school all day, and then spent four or five hours trying to figure out strategy. Often the meetings are to prepare statements and papers like the one 2 Tall delivered in Baton Rouge.

Shakoor remembers, "At least half of Fyre Youth was not living with a parent. They'd gotten home to New Orleans however they could. One time I'm taking the same kid to the Lower Nine, another time Uptown somewhere, another time to Gentilly. And it really broke me up when I was getting ready to lock up the Homecoming Center for the night, and I asked one young lady, 'Which way are you going?' And I could tell she wasn't sure. There was just this long pause while she tried to figure out where she's gonna sleep that night. A seventeen-year-old. And it became really clear this is not the way things are supposed to be."

Just like everything, it seems, in New Orleans, we take one step, and then another. The next thing you know we are traveling through doorways we never expected to traverse. But we are standing with the youth, and whatever their fate is or becomes we go there with them.

Now Fyre Youth are being targeted by teachers and security guards because of reforms they are successfully demanding like the reduction in the number of guards or better qualified teachers. They begin to come under different forms of intimidation in school. Because of all the time they are devoting to organizing, their grades are beginning to slip, and some want to use this to expel them.

So with the help of an Episcopal congregation in Naples, Florida, Trinity-by-the-Cove, and Episcopal Relief and Development, we set up after-school tutorial resources. We expect to offer these to the fifteen or twenty core group members of Fyre Youth, but suddenly the numbers mushroom. Next thing we know about fifty young people are coming to the door every afternoon.

"And then," Shakoor remembers, "the word got around the neighborhood and kids of all ages started showing up. We tried for a couple of days saying this was just for Fyre Youth. But how many times can you tell a child when they obviously have nothing to do, and nowhere to go, that they can't come in? So we changed that and started letting everyone in. And then we had a ministry for children that ranged from eight or nine years old to twenty."

Shortly before school concludes for the summer, Mary Fontenot from All Congregations Together arrives with a woman named Pastor Josie Philips of Say the Word Pray the Word Church. Pastor Josie has developed a relationship with the Children's Defense Fund to set up a summer Freedom School, but she does not have a location since her church is still destroyed. We agree to house her summer program.

The Children's Defense Fund is building on the history of several decades. Freedom Schools were originally developed in Mississippi and Alabama in the 1960s because of the obstacles that Jim Crow segregationists in the South were using to keep blacks from voting. Incredibly difficult questions would be thrown at blacks to prevent them from registering to vote. Freedom Schools were set up to train folks so they would be able to pass these onerous requirements.

Like our situation, the schools developed and became a way volunteers from colleges throughout the country could come to the South and participate in the movement by teaching people to read. Then a broader mission—teaching activism and citizen engagement—grew out of the emphasis on literacy, so that the Freedom Schools also became about handing on an understanding of what a citizen is supposed to be in a democracy.

Now in the summer of 2007 that heroic chapter is being brought forward, and Freedom Schools are being set up throughout New Orleans to deal with deficiencies in the education system. Pastor Josie will teach a love of reading, community service, and provide opportunities for field trips. The idea is to wrap children living in a distressed area in a bond of love, family, and community.

But the Freedom School can only enroll thirty-five children. So we decide to open Camp Ubuntu, naming our camp after the famous South African principle championed by Desmond Tutu. *Ubuntu* is what persons have and teach when they interact with others in ways that say, "You are a precious child of God." Lo and behold, we end up with ninety children from the community coming to the camp every day.

The steps continue, and with each step we are growing and learning. We not only come to know the children by name, and get to know their personalities, but we begin to be invited into their homes. This leads increasingly to a family-focused outreach developed by an outstanding Methodist pastor from Boston, visiting for the summer, named Vickie Williams. It is now we see that the children's situations are even worse than we ever thought.

"It was astounding to go into a small shotgun house and find as many as fifteen people living in the tiny space. You'd be stepping over little beds made of blankets and pillows on the floor as you tried to move through. I began to see," Shakoor explains, "how difficult their situations really were and how the children were forced to be parents themselves, taking on adult levels of responsibility at thirteen or fourteen years old. I continually wonder how they can do it and not be really angry. We have a few of our children who are boiling with rage, but the vast majority are just sweet, loving, caring kids."

Seeing and experiencing all of this for the first time in my life is emotionally demanding, bewildering, and I find myself swinging from highs of intense joy as I come to know these children as friends, to real pain and anguish over their circumstances. I am extremely grateful for Shakoor, who helps me understand that much of this kind of hardship is normative in parts of the black community, and one is taught as you are growing up mechanisms for coping. I am impressed by his resilience in dealing with these situations emotionally and probe to find out more about where that comes from in him. And so he shares with me his childhood story.

"I was born in Tuttwiler outside of Clarksdale, Mississippi. We were sharecroppers on a cotton plantation, and extremely poor. Sahara, my mother, only went to school when it rained. Otherwise you were out in the field. So she could barely read. I helped her learn to write and read as I was growing up. She had me, her eldest, when she was fourteen, and so we kind of grew up together.

"I left Mississippi when I was about five. My real father left to go to Detroit to find work in an auto plant. With the mechanization of agriculture you needed less farm labor. So it was always hard but it became even harder. He got a job at the Cadillac plant in Detroit. He was supposed to send for us but he forgot.

"My mother decided we would go find him, which was a big step. At that point she was eighteen or nineteen and never been outside of Tuttwiler. We really didn't have enough money to get to Detroit, so we were going to go to Buffalo, where my grandfather lived, get some funds and shoot across to Michigan. My grandfather had remarried after my grandmother had died. It was one of those Cinderella stories. The night we got there my step-grandmother threw us out. So we were forced to wander the streets of Buffalo homeless.

"We found an area, like every town at that time, where they were building a new highway to new suburbs through the black community. There were some blocks of abandoned houses on the edge of the neighborhood they call the Fruit Belt. So we kind of squatted there. Then my mother went out and found work at a diner. She was befriended at the diner by Fatima Aljuwani, the sister of my stepfather-to-be.

"So I've been there. I know about what these children are living through, and having to take on larger adult roles. I remember my mother was afraid of rats. As they were tearing down each one of those abandoned houses the rats would move from building to building, and we were the last house on the block. These were *rats*—huge. I think that's how I developed my insomnia. My mother would work all day, and I would stay up all night fighting rats.

"I kept a little axe and I would just try to keep them out of our bed. I got to where the slightest noise would wake me up. I remember one night I killed about eight of them. Then one night we were visiting my grandmother-to-be, eating at the table and I started dozing off. She asked why so I told her.

"She had this huge cat named Midnight, and she gave Midnight to me. Then I could get some rest because that cat was ferocious, although he did have a bad habit of bringing the dead rats and putting them in the bed. That was Big Mama who gave me Midnight. I was six."

I've been trying to understand what Big Mamas are. Everyone talks about before the storm how they were fixtures in the neighborhood, but I've never heard of this before. People keep talking about how since the storm the absence of Big Mamas has left a gaping hole in the landscape of the community. I want to learn more.

Shakoor says, "It's a black thing. They used to call my grandmother Big Mama. My mother was Little Mama. With age you had to give respect. My grandmother lived around the corner. She took two blocks one way and my mother took two blocks the other way, and they ruled it.

"Little Mama was a fighter for education. She'd say, 'I can't help you with your homework, but I'm going to make sure you get a decent education.' So she was at every PTA meeting. Once my mother remarried and we moved, right next door to us lived Clara Mose, who became my mother's best friend. She was one of two or three people on our block who actually had a college education. So they were like the S.W.A.T. Team, Little Mama, Clara, and Big Mama was out there too. They went to anything that had to do with education. Clara was extremely articulate and Mother was her enforcer. They found any young person on the block who was being short-changed and they became their advocate.

"And I had friends whose parents were alcoholics or drug addicts or whose family was in disarray and we kind of absorbed them. Sahara would fight for them in school and they would come to our house and eat, so she was the mother for the whole block. That's what a Big Mama is.

"There were two things that helped me as I was growing up that I try to pass along. I was taught an understanding of black history that the average black youth or adult did not have at the time. I was quite clear about my heritage long before it became the practice. The Aljuwanis were a clan. My grandfather, Ali Aljuwani had been a Garveyite in the 1920s, following the legendary Black Nationalist Marcus Garvey.

"Being practicing Muslims in the 1950s, we were incredible oddballs and we caught a lot of hell. There were times I was beaten by my teachers for no other reason than not being Christian. I was one of the smallest boys in my class, but I was also always one of the smartest. I was in the toughest schools in Buffalo. There were only two or three smart girls and me. So I had to learn to stand up.

"So the other thing I try to pass along is when you are a minority you have to figure out how not to be a minority. I learned that you need friends. You need support. I had to get some troops. So I developed an organizing style where I would find one of the toughest guys and I would help him with his schoolwork and then he would help back me up. And that is how I began to be an organizer."

I am really coming to know and understand an entirely new culture, as Nell would say, "on its terms," thanks to the work, the children, and Shakoor. Together we begin to parade every person with a passion for and understanding of the dynamics in the schoolrooms and in the lives of our youth into the office to meet Bishop Jenkins.

One such person, a former Freedom Rider, Jerome Smith (aka Big Duck), appears at my door, just down the street from John Mac, one night. He comes to ask to meet "this Bishop Jenkins." Then he launches into a very moving kind of extemporaneous sermon. He talks about his parents, and his father telling him as a boy, "You may be poor and you may be black, but you aren't dirty and you aren't dumb." How painstakingly his parents educated him. He tells me about being beaten and jailed with Dr. King. He says, "I believe every child is the Christ child. And I have a vision for the children. I want to talk to this bishop I keep hearing about. I believe that you are sincere."

It's a pairing that causes quite a stir in town, as Jerome is an uncompromising champion of the young African American males of the city, and can be quite fierce at times. He has led thousands of youth on City Hall in his day, and now his children are scattered all over the country. The Bishop and Big Duck are seen more and more often taking off together in the bishop's car. One day I ask Bishop Jenkins what the two of them are up to and discover that Jerome is helping him like Shakoor is helping me.

The bishop says, "My work with Jerome is life-giving to me. He has kind of adopted me as a mentoring project. He is very patient with me, which is not necessarily Jerome's long suit—patience. He strikes fear into the hearts of a lot of people. But he is mentoring me and helping me to see things from a perspective I would not otherwise see them. An example of that that stands out in my mind has been our trips to the FEMA camp, Renaissance Village, in Baker, Louisiana. And the folks in Baker, their mayor, their city council, have been awfully good to our displaced brothers and sisters, but the situation they are in is terrible.

"One day Jerome and I went up there, and as usual we got lost. And we were driving around the countryside and looking. And we passed a school bus. And Jerome said, 'You know, Bishop, these displaced black children living in trailers get on this school bus and they go to Baker to a good school and so forth. But they look around and they don't see any white children on this school bus. Were no white kids displaced in this?'

"And of course the answer to that question is terribly deep. But one of the things Jerome is doing is giving me the insight of a black child. He is so committed to children. So what are we doing? We are establishing a couple of safe houses to protect children from each other. We sponsored the entire summer program for Tambourine and Fan, which is a very positive thing. We have been involved at the St. Thomas Clinic and the coffee shop they've opened in there. We're working with the

Sylvan Learning Center to get some of the Tambourine and Fan youth into their program and I hope to move Sylvan to the Treme Center Jerome runs. Jerome continues to travel to meet with displaced youth in the diaspora, because he believes in the African American, Afro-Caribbean experience here that is just different from Atlanta or Houston. And Jerome really believes in the value of that.

"At the same time we are trying to find a way to introduce some inner city African American youth to some of our Episcopal boarding schools, at least to open their eyes to a different way of being in the culture. I go with Jerome and I meet a group of black children and I realize I am the only white male they have ever had a positive interaction with. I bet you experience this at St. Luke's with the kids there. You're the only white female they've met that they've ever had a positive interaction with. I'm not there to judge. I'm not there to scold. I'm not there to say, 'Sit down!' or arrest you, but to take an interest in your life.

"There is for me a deeply personal aspect to the experience I'm having with Jerome Smith and it is transformative and life-giving. The work Jerome does is heroic. But he's not the only hero in the city.

"I am also grateful to Raynard Sanders and Dave Dennis. I struggle with the severe interpretation that some are intent on destroying the public school system. That is somehow almost beyond belief. But it does seem that the system of intentional under-education continues no matter who is at the helm. The system of seeing education as a matter of self-interest rather than community improvement is beyond moral comprehension, and that did not begin recently. It's an old pattern, maybe an effect of colonialism.

"But the idea of using education to prepare an unskilled workforce is morally repugnant. The idea of withholding good education from children to keep them in their place is beyond moral redemption. And I think that Raynard and Dave are standing heroically for a different vision of what education in this state ought to be. When education becomes a tool for the perpetuation of parallel societies there is a huge problem there. When the affluent community can say, 'I don't have to care about public education because I can afford something better,' we've totally lost that idea I keep coming back to of Rabbi Sachs's—common fate.

"I think Louisiana's educational failures have not simply been failures of omission but at times have been sins of commission—'Let's keep 'em down.' What we've realized in our work is that keeping them down—we are them. We are they.

"And theologically, we are created with a divine dignity that can't be squared with that attitude. Like St. Athanasius said, 'God became man so that man might become God.' A person is an end and not a means to an end. Their life can't be used for some menial purpose.

"I don't think that any longer there is an intentional motivation. It may be there in some but I don't know that. Perhaps in a former colonial mindset there was the idea that we needed an *undermensche* 'to work the place' so to speak. It could be a systemic pathology that we have inherited. If so we don't worry about it much.

"If there is such a thing as a multi-generational transmission of anxiety and stress and even trauma, and I personally think there is, we have yet to even deal with the trauma that goes back and has been compounded for four hundred years. And the indignity that was heaped on human beings—men torn from their families and put in chains. The indignity of women being torn from their children and used as sex objects. No matter who was doing it. And I don't doubt there is a multi-generational transmission of that trauma. I don't doubt there is a multigenerational transmission of trauma in families who were involved on the other side of that issue. The more I think about this, the more I think we are going to need to find a way to deal with that. Deep down I believe multi-generational trauma and pathologies are controlling some of our behavior, and we're going to have to find a way to begin to deal with that."

———

I like talking to Shedrick White, a teacher at John Mac, about all this because he is in the classroom with the kids every day. On the subject of some kind of invisible, unnamed pathology, Shed puts it this way, "I don't know whether it be subconscious or whatever it is—but it leave the youth out."

He agrees there is a great deal of trauma, and it started before the storm. "Lots of kids been through it before," he says. "Not in terms of natural disaster but you had a lot of family disaster—a lot of single-parent homes, a lot of incarcerated parents. The murder rate and the violence that was around. The drugs and the addictions that was around.

So kids was already prepared to deal with stuff like that and not become completely unraveled. They had experience dealing with disaster.

"But they haven't talked about it enough. It's still huge for teenagers to be accepted among their peers. It's not cool to be reacting, and if it's not cool to my peers I might try to hide it."

Shedrick however is a very creative teacher, and while some at John Mac have yet to find a way to establish order in the classroom, Mr. White has found a method for teaching the kids and helping them with some of their life challenges at the same time.

"That is why I started the poetry to provide that outlet for the kids and even more to teach them about coping. A lot of people have only learned one way and that's to hold everything inside. It's not healthy. It's gonna come out some kinda way. So they need to learn coping mechanisms.

"I think they need to write. They need to write to get some of it out. It's a way to get a conversation goin'. It's cool now because the Hip Hop artist, for a generation of youth, has provided a format for a message. Hip Hop is just a more rhythmatic type poem. The kids will write poetry on their own. In 2005 I knew kids who were sittin' on whole books of poetry already. So I use this approach in my classroom and I think if we had some kind of citywide outlet for the kids to write and recite you'd see the kids come out."

We begin to work with Shed on realizing his dream, which he was close to achieving at the time Katrina hit.

"What I'd love to see is a weekly venue with the kids expressin' themselves. I think it would help with the overall violence because the kids consider the violent crimes, crimes of expression. If they knew how to properly express themselves it wouldn't come out as violence. So I think, with the number of kids I believe would participate, I think we'd see our murder rate drop. And I think we'd see participation from probably five year olds to seniors in school to be honest with you.

"All they are strugglin' with, the embarrassment of being behind developmental wise, that kind of shame. It can cause you to act out. Just bein' behind causes some of the kids to act out. I remember one of the first songs in the history of Hip Hop was a song called, 'It's a jungle sometimes. Makes me wonder how I keep from goin' under.' And the whole song is a bitter picture of the inner city.

"You see, New Orleans is like an American refugee camp. You see, this city, to be honest with you, is where you spend the least amount of money on the school system, where you spend the most in the prison system. We spend the least amount of money on youth programs and incarcerate youth at the fastest rate in the nation. When everybody else's infant mortality went down, Louisiana was the only one that went up. Pet mortality led the nation. I fall out when I saw that.

"We are the largest municipal jail. No other city jail keeps people longer than they do at central lock up. In most cities it is a six-month sentence. But nowhere else in the country do you see people in a city jail for eight and ten years. So it's a lot of sittin' ducks here.

"Like before they had the sophisticated weather systems. How did they know dangerous storms were comin'? Well what would happen was that the ducks who could fly would leave. The ducks that couldn't had to stay there and weather the storm, hence the term sittin' duck.

"We have a fearless, courageous generation of youth out there. They just need to be pointed in the right direction and be part of some kind of movement. They'll join. We've seen it with Fyre Youth Squad. People just waitin'. Just waitin' for a call. I've found poetry is a great motivational tool and a tool of inspiration to put out that call. In the community with the kids this poem is the signature piece. This is how it goes."

Suddenly Shedrick White assumes his persona as the bard of the black youth of the city, and begins to tell their story in rhyme, in terms they can hear, relate to, and understand. As I listen I feel like Bishop Jenkins says he feels in the company of Jerome Smith. I'm being given a chance to view the world through the eyes of young black New Orleanian males.

Shedrick begins. "I think most of the violence is faulted. A brother's tryin' to prove whose hood is the hardest. This poem right here is my vision of two boys havin' a conversation about just that: "Whose Hood Is the Hardest?"

The black struggle is not over so for me it's still crunch time,
Was the thought that ran through my mind as I passed the school during lunchtime.
And it was ghetto-fab y'all.
Instead of jumpin' rope, the girls were backin' it up.
And instead of playin' ball, the boys were on the hood of the car,
Because the truancy hackin' 'em up.
Now you woulda really thought they was grown if you'd a heard
   these children conversin'.

I mean you woulda really thought they was grown if you
    coulda heard
How these kids was cursin'.
On this particular day in my life, I really must make mention.
It was a conversation between two boys that really caught
    my attention.
I know I shouldn't be nosey—or maybe I should 'cause
The topic of the conversation was how hard each other's
    hood was.
Now the first one had to be from the project or at least that's
    what I assumed,
Because he said, "To live in my court I either gotta pick up a
    gun or pick out a tomb."
Then he talked about how he hit the block and helped his uncle
    sell rock.
Or how they beat up people with G-Nikes because him and their
    click only wear Reeboks.
Then he talked about how they be hittin' hustles and pullin' capers.
He said, "Man my hood's so notorious they don't even deliver
    the mornin' papers."
Said, "It's rough like that when you're livin' in the 'jects.
The only reason the mailman comes through is because he gotta
    deliver them checks."
He said, "The weak ones we punk 'em, the cowards we
    scare 'em.
They be so petrified they buy brand new Jordans and don't even
    wear 'em."
He said, "I was thirteen years old when I drunk my first Forty.
And fourteen years old when I stayed all night at my first party.
And fifteen years old when I sold my first dime.
And sixteen years old when I snorted my first line.
We bought it like that in my hood and we ain't never gonna
    stop that.
I know my hood's the hardest. Let me see you try to top that?

And the second boy replied by saying:
When I said my hood was hard I wasn't talkin' about thuggin'.
I was talkin' hard from hard times, that come from hard core
    strugglin'.

You see it's hard for us to eat at Houston's and Copeland's,
'Cause all we can afford is Church's.
And it's hard for us to get a Visa or Mastercard because all we
    have is the Louisiana Purchase.
Hard is how my daddy works, but he ain't make much cash.
The closest he came to pullin' out a credit card is when he pulled
    out his bus pass.
And it's hard for us to live in peace, 'cause people gossip and
    keep mess.
And it's hard to get to the next grade 'cause they done made it
    hard to pass the Leap Test.
Uh-oh, look it. The bell ringin. Said, bro' I gotta go.
But we can talk after school if you want to discuss this some mo'.
But I'm gonna leave you with this, 'cause I don't think I've said
    enough.
You see, I'm talkin' about life bein' hard
While you talkin' about a hood bein' rough.
After talkin' with my Pops I know this for a fact.
We wouldn't be talkin' about whose hood is the hardest
If we both wasn't black.
And once we realize this we should study to be the smartest.
Because life for black people in any ghetto is always gonna
    be the hardest.

As soon as I hear Shed recite, I know we have found a man with a calling. He and Shakoor begin to huddle and devise a plan to organize youth across the city through the magic of Shedrick's poetry. The concept is to take youth who are viewed by many in the city as the crux of our social problems, and surround them with the kind of formation and nurture they need to become leaders of the solution.

———

It's difficult to describe what it feels like to be living in this world knowing how much you've been given in life. To have had so many incredible life experiences, to have traveled to so many places, and had so many beautiful things, a first-class education, and a hand up getting started in one's career, and then to see how tiny the options are for our brilliant, gifted, loving, eager children.

The smallest things are huge treats: a ride in the car singing to the radio, driving uptown is even more exciting. We go shopping at Walmart, and Noogie in true New Orleans parlance exclaims, "We done *made* some groceries!" It's an experience just loading the car with shopping bags of food. Making snowballs (as they call snow cones in New Orleans) is Charles's forte. Each one is a multi-colored, multi-flavored work of art. He is itching to buy a machine and go into business.

The opportunity to go see a movie sends our kids into orbits of ecstasy. A weekend sleepover at the church's big blue Urban Ministry Center is an over-the-top adventure. Everyone competes over who gets to help make pancakes for breakfast, tuna fish sandwiches for lunch, and spaghetti and meatballs for dinner. The worst part is when one little girl cries and begs me not to make her go back home.

If I had all the resources I really need in this work, first priority would be the basics: a nutritional diet, medical check ups, a mattress to sleep on at night. A house the children and their families could live in comfortably. A car for the parents instead of a bicycle.

Next tier of my wish list is all about education. I want to introduce the kids to college campuses. I want to start education funds for their future learning opportunities. I dream of building them a school. I dream of creating a cultural center for them in a fabulous old defunct plantation house that has a big For Sale sign in front. I dream of shopping with them to create for each a library of books about the things they are really interested in learning. I couldn't do science or math, but there are lots of things I could teach them about English and history or religion.

I wrack my brain to think of how we could enroll Eric in a great drama program, because he's a natural-born actor. Of finding Noogie a better math tutor, because as he says when he's playing craps with lightening speed like nothing I've ever seen, "That Miss Courtney is why I am so great at math." I want to make sure Alfelicia's incredible writing talent is nurtured. The list is endless. But for now I must do what can be done with meager resources. And although it isn't nearly what I know I could do, we have a great time together doing what we can.

It really does something to my heart when Shakoor calls from the road after taking the kids to the Church Youth Camp out in the country one day and says, "Your children want to say hello. They missed you today." Or when one of the mothers of six children, living on $500 in food stamps and a $220 Social Security Income check monthly—that's it—says, "Thank God, Miss Courtney, you didn't have children, because we need your help." Or when Eric appears at my front door one day, kind of bashful, and says, "You know, at first I thought you was an uppy, uppy preppy girl. But turns out you's cool." It is a great gift to feel those secret moments when trust is born happening between us. "I'm so honored that you feel that way," I tell Eric. There is no bigger gift he could give me.

The person who is a godsend in developing ways to support the children and their families is Vickie Williams. She keeps my maternal instincts in check and reminds me every day that the goal is to empower the parents and the guardians to do what they need and want to do for their children. The issue is not a lack of love or concern. It is a lack of skills and resources.

Most became parents when still in their teens, and as a result never finished high school. This minimized career options. There wasn't much life experience to bring to setting up household, never mind financial resources. Folks band together with relatives taking turns with childcare, cooking, sharing whatever they have between them. Big extended families living within a few blocks move back and forth between houses, in and out of the screen doors on their porches, kids playing in the street, doing their homework at Grandma's, watching TV at Auntie's house, going to church together on Sunday.

This is the sort of thing about neighborhood life in the black community the bishop is talking about when he says to me one day, "In my experience and my life there are things I so envy about the black community. Families all across this country seem to be so challenged—none more so than the black family in the inner city. But there's still a strong sense of the importance of family. One of the great tragedies of Katrina is that our patterns of family living where we kind of lived in family blocks in this city were destroyed."

It is going to be arduous to help families put this back together again. It's not the sort of thing programs can replace or money alone can buy. The secret, as one Big Mama says, is "everybody belongs to everybody." Residing in the hood, I am getting a taste of what it's like to live this way. You could not find any lifestyle more opposite than my former Upper East Side existence. As Vickie says to me one day, "Girl, you done gone from rich to poor!" And the two of us "fall out" because it is the God's honest truth.

One day Nell and I are talking about how one sustains this kind of work, and as usual she says something I think is very wise. I ask her, "What do you think it takes to stick with it?" She says, "Well, frankly, I still have some internal conflict that I chose to come home and left the work in Nigeria, but kinship won.

"And I think part of what it takes to stick with it is having the work be about more than an issue, and about more than a concern or even a vision. But having the relationships that keep you fed and keep you in it. As an outsider you have to develop those, and as an outsider you always have a choice to leave."

Perhaps it's the writer in me, but one of those intriguing friendships that is keeping me hopeful and keeping me in this is my new relationship with Shedrick White. He has definitely made my list of heroes in the city. It is really exciting to think what he and Shakoor might achieve as a team with Shakoor's organizing skills and Shed's poetry club concept. I can't wait to introduce him to Bishop Jenkins.

I ask him how all of this began and he says, "I wanted to connect with the youth and I saw if I really want to be effective I gotta come this route." So Shed taught himself to write the poems. "It's like a motivational speaker doin' a poem. I do it that way because I think the kids find it a little more magical if you can put something together like that. They can really and truly be amazed. Some of the kids feel kind of special that you sat down and wracked your brains and put in that time to write a message that is just for them. They know it isn't something I can go to the club with. It's just for them."

Shed says the youth of the city are ready to do something big. They're just waiting for the call. And it sounds as though he really has a way with boys who are turning toward violence out of pure frustration and rage. We know underneath the anger is the pain. He tells me a story that happened before the storm that I can't get out of my mind.

"Crime Stoppers got a tip there was gonna be some gun play at Kennedy [High School]. The superintendent didn't call the police. He called me. He separated the groups and each sat in a room. There was Seventh Ward, St. Bernard Projects versus the football team. That particular time I sat in the room with the guys from St. Bernard. At first they was bein' real defiant or whatever. But when I left, some one of these gangsters was followin' me to my car sayin', 'Mr. White, could you do one more poem for me and my boys?' And the principal said when I left that day he had no more violence between the two sides.

"So when I went back it dawned on me to film what I did with the football team. And that led to a contract with the Safe and Drug Free Schools program called 'Non-Violence or Non-Existence' named after Dr. King's phrase. And we were going to pilot the poetry club in all the schools, but then the storm came. The slogan of the poetry club was gonna be 'I gotta write to bear arms.' And there is a poem that goes with it I was gonna use to introduce the program to the kids."

I keep a pen with me because I gotta write to bear arms
Meanin' my pen is my weapon
And it's kept in my pocket.
When I feel inspired I pull it out and cock it
And do a drive-by on paper.
I can kill you with a gun but with a pen it's much safer
I gotta write to bear arms so I won't become a menace,
And you'll never see me in the Pen doin' a sentence
Only with a pen doin' a sentence
I gotta a write to bear arms
And if I don't I'm gonna pick up a Nine
And if I do, I'm gonna pick up some time.
So instead I'm gonna pick up a rhyme.
Because my creative clip is screamin' empty me
So I sweep streets with metaphors and burn blocks with similes.
I hold you up at tongue point hopin' you will follow
Offerin' you a few tips hopin' that my points are not hollow—see
I gotta write to bear arms and I'm hopin' that you do it.
When you express yourself the right way trust me, it's
     therapeutic.
So you should write to bear arms because it's really not that hard
Plus you'll feel more power because everyone knows
that the pen is mightier than the sword.

## CHAPTER 9

# SILENCE IS VIOLENCE

———◆———

IN DECEMBER 2006 AND JANUARY 2007, THE DEATHS OF DINERRAL
Shavers and Helen Hill spark shock, grief, and fury throughout the
city. But the work and life commitments of both victims cut particularly close to the bone for those of us working with youth in distressed
neighborhoods. We identify with both Dinerral and Helen, as well as
with Helen's husband, Paul, who survives three gunshot wounds. All
three are particularly known for their community-mindedness, their
voluntarism, and a deep commitment to what the new New Orleans
might be.

It's a tragic holiday season. Six people have been shot in one day,
twelve in one week. Shavers was shot on the Thursday after Christmas, and Hill one week later. The newspaper headline in the *Times
Picayune* reads, "Killings Bring the City to Its Bloodied Knees." And
it is true. As if we have not yet been brought low enough.

Dinerral Jevone Shavers Sr., born March 19, 1981, a twenty-five-
year-old Civil Sheriff Deputy, and a founding member of the Hot 8
Brass Band, was known for his snare drum, and as a prolific songwriter
with a knack for uplifting lyrics. His song "Get Up" was about making things better in this world. "My people keep the peace, keep the
murder rate down," he wrote. He believed, "If a kid has a horn in his
hand, he won't have a gun." And so in his spare time, he founded and
directed the marching band at L. E. Rabouin Senior High School.

Eighty young people in the band revered Dinerral as a father figure to many and a role model to all. His life ended when he was shot in his car driving with his wife and child.

The second is the murder of Helen Hill, a thirty-six-year-old film-maker and graduate of Harvard. Shortly before 6:00 a.m. a gunman enters the white double shotgun house where Helen, her husband, Paul Gailiunas, and their two-year-old son, Francis, live. The intruder fatally shoots Helen in the neck, and pumps three shots into Paul, while he is clutching their son near the couple's front door. Gailiunas survives. Again, the victims are known for their sincere commitment to helping others. Helen worked with challenged youth. Paul, a physician, worked with the community-based Daughters of Charity Health Center, giving low-income people a level of care and attention money cannot buy.

One grief-stricken friend recalls expressing to both one day, "You're exactly the kind of people I want to move to New Orleans and start a family." Helen grew up in South Carolina, Paul in Canada. For many of us who have come to New Orleans, as well as many native New Orleanians, it is as though our hope in being a new kind of community has been shot down.

Saundra Reed recalls, "It scared the beejeezus out of all the white people in New Orleans because the violence had been happening in black communities for a long time, but now it had seeped out of our own messy places. With the percentage of blacks and whites skewed toward whites for the first time in generations, a lot of people were beginning to understand, 'I'm not isolated from it anymore. It is happening everywhere.' And that is because our demographics have changed so much. It got to the point that the conversation on how to stop the violence was becoming very, very broad.

"It was decided there was going to be a march to City Hall to really cry out to our elected officials about—like they said in the movie *Network*, 'We're sick and tired and we're not going to take it anymore.' All kinds of energies got stuck together. It was very organic. That's how I first talked to Shakoor. I talked to him for maybe eight or ten days before I ever laid eyes on him. He was promising to be able to deliver some support for this march. We were discussing the idea of marching from one spot—because that is how the police wanted it to go—a designed little march where we politely go, and get to City Hall and say, 'Y'all make us sick,' and then it's over.

"But the people had a different point of view. And Shakoor said, with his place in ACT, there were other people who were interested in joining energies. And that he had spoken to the bishop of the Episcopal Church and he was also willing to march. Well I'd worked with Nell Bolton and some others, I call them Episcopal angels, in some other community work, and we'd all been in the UNOP planning and Community Congress. We'd also worked on community benefits agreements. But I had never worked with them in a way sanctioned by the administration of the Episcopal Church. It was more like we were neighborhood partners. When Shakoor said he understood the bishop wanted to come I just said, 'Anybody who want to come we're gonna be over here.'"

On the morning of Thursday, January 18, about 7:30 a.m., my cell phone rings and it is Bishop Jenkins. As soon as I see who is calling I know it is about the march. It turns out that because this is Charles Jenkins's first public protest demonstration the bishop wants to check with me about what he should wear. I affirm his instinct to wear the color that symbolizes his status as a bishop. "I think I should look purple today, what do you think?" "Oh yes," I say, "the purpler you can be today the better." The next question also carries symbolic weight. Where should we march from and with which body of residents?

This is a loaded question. One victim being mourned today is black, one white. Some in the black community say that the reason the city is finally up in arms is because the violence has felled a prominent white woman. As a whole the city has never mobilized on the issue of violent killings before. Yet young black males like Eric and Noogie and Floyd, and all our dear ones at St. Luke's, are being killed weekly. So are the youth so beloved by Jerome Smith. It's impossible to work with the children without holding your breath and saying your prayers every night that they will remain safe and not be drawn into the pull of the street.

I am living in a neighborhood where the sound of gunshot fire is commonplace. The blue glare of police lights throws an eerie cast on the walls of my home every night. You can feel the fact that random violence is near. But that does not haunt me like the thought that one of my children could fall at any time. The children live daily with the feeling we had in New York after the attack: that the next blow will fall any minute, that we are living in the sights of a gun, every day. And that is part of the problem. Living this way desensitizes you. Life eventually begins to appear cheap. Trauma becomes the norm.

As the words of one grief-stricken New Orleans mother posted on the Internet after the brutal shooting of her son and nephew in July 2005 demonstrate, many of these shootings are senseless acts that seem to be about the random release of rage:

> My son was running for his life and the gunman chased him at least a block and a half, and stood over him once he fell to the ground and shot him four more times, a total of seven times. The gunman was only fifteen, and the little guy he had with him was fourteen. Two weeks later when he was captured the police asked him the one question I feel I will never be satisfied with. That was, "Did you know these young men?" And he said, "No. They were just some nigga on the block." And when asked, "Well why did you kill them?" And he said, "Cause I felt like it." . . . I now come to you wanting to add myself to the Silence Is Violence organization. I feel that the murder of Mr. Shavers and Ms. Helen and my son were unnecessary. I do not doubt that this city needs to make a lot of changes from the highest to the lowest chain of command, but we have to get it right. We just have to get it right. Signed—A Brokenhearted Mother

It is a slap in the face to all the brokenhearted mothers that the white community is up in arms now for the first time, but true to form the mothers choose to rise above the wounding insult. Others have asked, "Should the black community join this march at all?" The subject has been debated at the grassroots level for ten days. Shakoor is one who has appreciated the principle held by many, but argued for full city-wide participation by all members of the community as a whole. After much debate, a consensus begins to emerge that what is at stake is too important to the city to be hindered by the injury. The idea emerges to organize and march by neighborhood, so that people are seen converging on city government from every direction, participating in the whole but also remaining distinct and identifiable. We all know which neighborhoods suffer most from violent crime, and the meaning of their participation carries unique significance. Approached this way, who you are marching with becomes symbolically important.

Bishop Jenkins lives on St. Charles Avenue, the most gracious boulevard in the city. On the riverside of St. Charles lies the Garden District, with its stately mansions and manicured yards. On the lakeside of St. Charles lies Central City, one of the most severely blighted neighborhoods in New Orleans, but one with an incredibly rich cultural heritage and history. There is no neighborhood in New Orleans more plagued or associated with violent black teenage crime than this one. And it is a stone's throw from the highest priced real estate in the entire state of Louisiana.

The Episcopal Cathedral, Christ Church, and the bishop's diocesan offices are on the Central City side of St. Charles. We face the Garden District, but Central City is our community. Our location is symbolic of the bridge we seek to build between neighbors. Our Jericho Housing Initiative is building affordable homes exclusively in the Central City community, and we have many ties there, especially since the bishop has became acquainted with several Central City pastors since the storm. But as far as the city's perceptions are concerned Episcopalians are associated with their predominant membership and that is anchored in the Garden District.

With whom will the Bishop of Louisiana march? The next call Bishop Jenkins places is to Shakoor.

"Bishop Jenkins called and joked with me, 'When are you going to get me arrested?' For him to even consider that as the Bishop of Louisiana surprised me, but I knew he was serious. I had thought he would march with white residents. I had no idea what might happen once thousands hit the streets. My instinct was to play it safe, but the Bishop said immediately, "No. We're not going to do that. I am marching from Central City." It hit me that I went more conservative than he did. I was so concerned for the institution that I forgot what was most prophetic. But the bishop did not forget. And from that day forward I always kept that in mind."

Saundra picks up the story from her sightline. "We met that morning at Pastor Raphael's church, and we had this great banner that we had made. All kind of energy was goin' on. Everybody came out—our police, our district folks—and everybody signed off on the banner. I was inside talking to Pastor Raphael about what a great public statement this banner was going to make. You were going to be able to see the people of Central City. Carol Beebel at Ashe Cultural Arts Center sent a drum corps so we'd have a really resounding beat to help us. And we were going to march straight up to City Hall.

"And *then* I saw Santa Claus comin'. There was a lovely man with his rosy cheeks and his shock of white hair dressed in the most beautiful purple cassock I've ever seen. And as I think about it right now I'm getting chills because he was so impressive. He was impressive because he was fearless in his gaze. He was amongst a gang of folks he had never laid eyes on before, but it was like, 'Well how you doin'? I'm Charles Jenkins.' And I was so impressed. I was floored. There was something about him. His sincerity was almost palpable."

Saundra says to the bishop, "I'd like to introduce you to Pastor Raphael."

"'Oh I'd love to meet 'im. Love to meet 'im," Jenkins says.

"So," Saundra describes, "we walk down the aisle of this really old Baptist Church, you know—with a slanted floor. I introduce the bishop to Pastor Raphael, another imposing person—six feet four, big broad-shoulder-kind-of-guy with this booming voice, and within seconds they were laughin' and hands shakin'. And it was like there was no stand-offishness. And so the bishop's humility showed forth immediately.

"Then we began to gather and we prayed together. I prayed, as did Pastor Raphael. I prayed for there to be nothing to go wrong in this day. And the bishop's humbleness of saying, 'Where do you want me to be? Do you want me at the end bringing up the rear?' It was like that. He didn't have any expectations like, 'I have come. Put me in my rightful position.' He didn't have any of that at all. He was very, very different."

Saundra ends up in an automobile. As she explains, "I had to get to City Hall so that when the marchers came I could make sure there was a place for the Central City folks to be, and I also had to speak as I was part of the program. So I was up on the podium lookin' out and as the pace of the drum came, the pace of the drum, I could feel it. The pace of the drum came up Loyola Avenue. And the crowd began to whisper, 'Here comes Central City! Here comes Central City!' There were hundreds of us.

"Oh, oh, Courtney! Because the bishop's tall and he's a big man, and he was all in purple, he was the one who you could see. And you could see him walking with his staff and the flags of the church waving, and you could hear the drum. It was a sea of people—six thousand—who turned their heads to look. Central City was like a stream and the crowd pushed over to one side and made way for us to flow in. And I had a chance to speak to the bishop afterwards and he was very pleased to have been able to be a part of that."

Bishop Jenkins says, "The march was certainly a very symbolic day for the city. And I was not an organizer. My role was to be a participant. I thought it was important to follow the leadership of Pastor

Raphael and the organizers. We didn't need to be a leader that day but to begin to stand publicly for the rights and dignity and the safety of all. That seemed very important."

The bishop is humble, so it seems he does not fully appreciate what it means to the people of the city to see him participate in the march as he has chosen to do. In a very public yet quiet way January 18, 2007, becomes another landmark date. It is the day that Charles Jenkins first displays at a municipal level this new sense of "we" that he is beginning to embody.

The same spirit of prophetic witness is bubbling up in many places and taking interesting forms. A deacon in the Episcopal Church, Elaine Clements, doesn't participate in the march that day, but the murders horrify her. It is particularly disturbing that other than the day of the march no one seems to be making much of a fuss about these killings. The names of murder victims show up on the second or third page of the second section of the newspaper, unless multiple victims are killed at once or the victim is someone prominent. It seems to Elaine that the loss of these lives is generally being dismissed. It is as if those who have lost their lives are not actually human beings.

Elaine approaches Fr. Bill Terry, rector of St. Anna's, and says, "I am really concerned about this. It doesn't seem anybody really cares. But how do you solve murder? It's huge. It has roots in failed education, and drugs, and trauma. How do you solve that?"

Fr. Terry believes in a principle he learned from Fr. Daniel Berrigan. "The charism of social justice has more to do with the act than with the outcome. There are things we can do, and to do something is so much better than to do nothing." Terry and Clements discuss the problem.

"In New Orleans we tend to reduce murder to numbers. We focus on the crime rate. So one thing we could do would be to focus on the human dynamic," Terry suggests.

One parishioner chimes in, "We ought to be marching on the mayor's office every week." Then Elaine's husband suggests, "Well, when you go you ought to take something." Elaine thinks, "A rose." So they start—two people going to the mayor's office every week, carrying a rose for each person who has been murdered in the city during that time.

To do this Elaine has to keep track of the names. She begins a scrapbook with clippings of newspaper articles, some from the national press, and obituaries, and they keep the album in the entrance of the church, by the front door, so it is seen as soon as people enter. At the front of the scrapbook is a running list of names and ages and how the person was shot, a photograph, so that as Elaine says, "They take on personhood and become real and human."

Fr. Terry begins to think about the Vietnam Memorial—the wall in Washington, D.C. with all the names of U.S. soldiers who fell in service. The congregation already has the list, so it is decided to create a wall on the exterior of St. Anna's, which will list each name, the person's gender, and age, and do so in a location on Esplanade Avenue where everyone driving by can see.

The congregation begins to pray for the victims and the perpetrators and all the people in public service who are responsible for peace and safety including the mayor, the police chief, and the district attorney. The ministry begins to grow and the outcomes are unforeseen.

It's a rainy Friday morning when Fr. Terry unfolds his morning paper sitting out on his porch and exclaims with some surprise to his wife, "Look, Vickie! The murder board is on the front page." By noon the parish administrator calls to say that the priest has received thirteen calls from the parents of victims who want to speak with him.

Bill Terry begins to make call after call. Some of the parents would like him to visit them in person. Some would like to come to the church. He makes a promise to the mothers who express over and over, "Thank you for not forgetting my baby." Fr. Terry says, "They will never be forgotten."

Bill says, "I've never had a day in my life like that day. After thirteen calls I couldn't take it anymore. I just broke down and cried."

Relationships are forming. St. Anna's, a working class church in the inner city, is becoming known as a voice for the poor, for the forgotten. Soon other congregations want to partner. St. Andrew's in uptown begins to take the same sort of bouquet of roses, each with a victim's name and a statement that this was a child of God, beloved by mothers, fathers, sisters, brothers, children, to the chief of police. The notes say we are praying for these victims by name and for their families and for the perpetrators, and for you. The folks at Silence Is Violence, who organized the march, are thinking of beginning to take a similar bouquet to the city's district attorney each week.

As Anderson Cooper on CNN, and then FOX national news, and ABC's *Dateline* and numerous other national media outlets begin to pick up the story, churches in other cities start to call and ask how they might begin extensions of the ministry.

Both Terry and Clements are encouraged, for both agree that not only the people in this city, but the people of this country need to be convinced that urban violence is a heartbreaking sociological phenomenon. "It is a plague, a twenty-first century holocaust in the United States. It's everywhere," says Terry.

The Reverend Susan Gaumer is passionate about her congregation's partnership in this ministry. "We are also praying that a national conversation could begin on crime. What we need to do is end it. Sadly there is a racist element to this. Some people do not care because they perceive this as being a black on black problem. But we pray for each person by name and the deep sense of tragedy over their deaths touches us. We feel increasingly close to those whose lives have been destroyed.

"The other day we had a bank robbery across the street. There was an AK47 lying in the middle of the street. The children in our school prayed for the perpetrators of the crime to find a better way. High crime invites more crime. Brazen crime invites more brazen crime. That is the dynamic in our city and it is awful.

Susan believes what I am coming to believe the longer I live and work in New Orleans. "It is because we have an underclass without the resources to maintain any sort of acceptable level of living that the unrest is so significant. I think it's going to take a social revolution in this city to deal with the root causes of crime. I hope it doesn't involve a race riot. But I think we have got to get more serious about not perpetuating an underclass in New Orleans, and I think that is our downfall. In rising crime we are looking at the results of not providing for the dignity of all.

"If we are going to be a civilized place we need to address straight on the issues of racism. They are critical here, even in a city where most of the African American community is not ghettoized to the degree it has been in other cities. And I am afraid sometimes we are regressing. We are doing a very scatter-shot approach to rebuilding. It is benefiting some and not all and that is apparent. The anger is going to boil over.

"We have to organize the churches. The social ideal, front and center, that the churches will have to lead is that God loves everyone. It is time for conversations in churches throughout the city on race. Until we do that we are not going to be able to deal with the systemic issues. Having an underclass is the way we have lived for generations. It is time for another Martin Luther King experience. Doing it in a non-violent way is going to be tricky, which is why the church leaders will be key.

"Katrina is the incident that brings up all the issues. New Orleans could become a flagship city in good governance and race relations. That's my dream. It's never far from my mind. I've chosen to stay the course. Our country needs to reform a great deal when it comes to social issues. Government favors the wealthy. The poor become poorer. That has got to change.

"The storm was a conversion experience for the bishop and the diocese. For the diocese to see where Jenkins is on these social issues— now that's grace! We had no idea. I hope it will lead to the conversion of the whole diocese, the whole city. Part of my hope comes from the fact that the bishop woke up."

As more people in the city become aware of his transformation, his conversion, Charles Jenkins assumes importance as a figure that represents all whose sense of compassion has been intensified and expanded by the storm. His humble and gracious "fearlessness," as Saundra described it, is our example, as we reach out to forge new and lasting friendships throughout this town.

The fact that the bishop has felt so inadequate and unprepared for this role makes him an even more powerful example and sacramental presence. For he is the first to say that whatever it is in him that we are drawn to, it does not stem from his own capabilities and strengths. He is always in touch with that dark night of the soul when he discovered such a deeply felt sense of contrition for his blindness in the past, but felt completely helpless to amend his life to the extent he saw was called for. Whatever fearlessness Charles Jenkins telegraphs with his eyes comes from beyond himself. And those who feel the pull of his example need to remember this part too. We are trying to empty ourselves to be given to something beyond ourselves.

Bill Terry says that he is observing "people that are active in the community joining the church for the first time." He says, "I think people are seeing that faith-based organizations are providing some of the most inspiring responses to Katrina of any of our institutions including government. It is as though there is a re-awakening of spiritual people who liked worshipping but thought of the church as a hypocritical institution. I think churches in New Orleans are rediscovering their spiritual identity. Members of the community decided we're not hypocrites. What we preach is what we do, and now they are excited about being part of a spiritual enterprise—worship coupled with praxis. It's a great combination."

However, all do not agree or like what Bishop Jenkins appears to be doing, and he has told me this is one of the most difficult crosses for him. "The bewilderment of people at what we're trying to do here, especially many of my longtime friends. There is a sense of alienation and disappointment from people I've known a long time about what we're doing and that saddens me. Still I feel propelled to move forward even more intentionally. I don't like to disappoint people, but we are disappointing many. I would like to be better at being able to invite others into the significance of what is happening here."

But the bishop says that he does not pray for "God to free me of this. That prayer has not crossed my lips. I ask for guidance, and I ask for strength, and I ask for patience. God does not call the brightest and the best into specific situations. There are a lot of people out there more capable than I. But I am not praying to be allowed to move on from this. It is not time to lay this cross down yet."

A few weeks after the "Silence Is Violence" march, the diocese dedicates another Homecoming Center we have been preparing for almost a year. This one is called the Episcopal Urban Ministry Center and it is located in a big rambling Victorian house on the edge of Central City. The bishop reaches out to our new friend Saundra Reed and asks if she would join Pastor John Pierre of Living Witness Church of God in Christ in representing the residents of Central City at the opening ceremony.

Saundra's words are directed toward the idea of what it means to be neighbors, and I can think of no better community leader in the city of New Orleans to define for us the meaning of the term. Because of the bishop's participation in the march, the very foundation of this friendship between Saundra's organization, Central City Renaissance Alliance, and the diocese, is grounded in a powerful and symbolic experience of partnership. We have recognized in one another that sense of shared fate. Now we are beginning to build upon that. In her wonderfully evocative way of illustrating deep points, Saundra Reed says, "We are neighbors, and that means, Bishop Jenkins, you can come to my house any time you need to borrow a cup of sugar. Just knock on my door. But that also means that I can come to your house over there on St. Charles Avenue and borrow a cup of sugar from you too."

From that day forward, like with Jerome, the sight of these two figures, Saundra Reed and Charles Jenkins, moving in tandem in many parts of the city, will become another one of those surprising duos that catches people's eyes. Of similar height and build, one with her crown of dreadlocks tied up in African cloth, one with his neatly starched white pocket-kerchief and gold pectoral cross, they move in synch, whispering to each other as they bustle through meetings and rallies. They look as though they share a unifying secret.

People take delight in seeing them together, especially those who know how witty and kind, profound and jocular both these extraordinary leaders can be. "Don't they make a cute couple?" someone observes as they scurry out of a City Council meeting together. The whole row I'm sitting in bursts into giggles. True to their sense of humor, both play up the joke. Saundra takes to calling the bishop, "my boyfriend," and Jenkins returns the favor by dubbing Saundra, "my cup of sugar." It is such a welcome relief from all the struggle and tension when genuine mutual friendships and true collegiality break through the racial geographies that constrict our lives, and life for a minute begins to feel like that glorious gleeful playground of freedom I recall so wistfully from my time at St. Paul's in New York.

Soon Saundra becomes another one of our greatly loved and admired mentors. She begins my education on the topic of her community by showing me a wonderful documentary produced by Linda Usdin, funded by the Casey Foundation. It is a good introduction to the cultural flavor of the Central City neighborhood. The documentary interviews several generations and four different branches of the extended Reed family, reminiscing about the neighborhood they once knew, and reflecting on the challenges facing the neighborhood before the storm. In the film folks are remembering the days when the whole community gathered on Fridays and Saturdays, when Poppa Yam got everybody out to clean up the yard in the morning, and threw a huge fish fry in the evening—a feast of shrimp and oysters for everybody every weekend.

Children played in the street, games like Pitty Pat and Five Up, while seniors watched the fun from their porches. Over and over different voices say the neighborhood has always been about family, older people helping kids, teaching love, spiritual guidance, the Ten Commandments. Ninety percent of neighborhood residents have responded to a survey saying that they view the church as a principle means of social support. Folks say that what neighborhood means to them is that it is "an environment where everybody loves me." As Saundra puts it, "That is our village. But it is not as extended a village as it once was."

This is because, since the 1950s, homeowners in Central City have been moving out and now 80 percent of the neighborhood is rental properties where landlords just come in to collect their money. Buildings are falling apart. Every empty lot used to house a well-established family. It is now a neighborhood where before the storm, 80 percent of children lived below the poverty line. Schools have declined, and as one neighbor says, "When kids stop learning they fill that void with something else." Central City has become the Ground Zero of black-on-black teenage violence in the city of New Orleans, and as the march from Pastor Raphael's church demonstrates, the community has had enough. Black and white signs dot the landscape saying just that in big block letters, "Enough!" and everybody in Central City knows exactly what those signs mean.

Like Treme, Central City is a neighborhood that is hard in both senses Shedrick White describes in his poem. It is a community whose residents struggle heroically with the hardship of poverty and to cope with that hardship they improvise like Irvin Mayfield says. They have taken what is bad and made it better by building a culture whose foundation is a broad, strong, and resilient extended family network.

But it is also a neighborhood where others, particularly angry and disaffected youth, have been preyed upon and diminished to the point that their lives have become not just hard, but rough—plagued with drugs and crime.

Like Treme, it appears the key to turning the tide in Central City has to do with creating healing strategies and positive outlets that intensively focus on the youth who are so embarrassed and frustrated, and filled with so much pain. Who haven't been sufficiently helped to cope with their struggle to survive in the strangulating wasteland of an increasingly blighted environment, and so turn to violent crime in order to make a statement that will be heard. Their pain has become our shared fate, and now through the relationship established with Saundra Reed, the Central City pastors, and the ACT congregations Shakoor has been working with, we are beginning to do something about it together.

As always we must be marching on multiple fronts. While we are working in communities to address the issues confronting those who have returned to the city, we must also continue to address the obstacles to coming home facing our neighbors still in exile.

An $11 billion federal program called "The Road Home" has been established to help displaced homeowners repair their houses and return. However, for some reason, people are not receiving the funds they need to come home. The program guidelines allow for up to $150,000 in assistance, depending upon the value and the damage to your house, but the stories that are beginning to come to our attention show the program is not working.

In his work as an organizer for ACT, Shakoor is told of one woman whose house was totaled. She has just received her Road Home award in the mail. She opened the envelope, filled with hope and relief, only to discover the check for a whopping $55.20. When she reads the amount the woman has a stroke.

This so incenses Shakoor that he sets for himself the task of researching the Road Home program inside out, to begin to get to the bottom of the issues homeowners are facing. He begins to talk to members at St. Luke's and discovers that the church treasurer, whose damage was appraised at $200,000, has received an award of $1,600 to repair her home. Marigold says to Shakoor, "That won't even buy the sheet rock."

Shakoor soon learns that a Washington, D.C. firm named ICF, with no experience administering this kind of program, has been given the contract. Shakoor discovers ICF is paid one dollar out of every ten of the $11 billion contract. He also discovers, reading the contract, there are no performance targets in the agreement whatsoever.

We begin to hear more and more stories like the $55.20 check. So, with our partners, All Congregations Together, we organize rallies at churches and ministers ask how many people in the church have applied. Shakoor reports, "People stand. Then we ask everyone who's received a check to sit down. Everybody is still standing. Then we find out there is no way to appeal inaccurate awards because ICF has no functioning appeal system."

For residents of the city that have savings and incomes that allow them to borrow significant sums of money, an alternative strategy for repairing their homes is available. They simply go to the bank and take out a loan. Neighborhoods composed of people who fall into this category begin to rebound visibly. But in neighborhoods of lower income people, of the elderly and retirees, homes continue to sit untouched but for the free volunteer labor supplied by citizens throughout the country.

Once again faith-based groups and organizers move into action to compensate for the fact that a private out-of-state company contracted by the government is getting rich off the misery of those who have suffered the most. We begin to use funds from our case management budget to advance resources to homeowners to buy their building materials. Then Katie Mears and her volunteers begin not only to gut but rebuild.

Many of the neighbors we help are homeowners like Ms. Cora who lives in Ponchartrain Park on the east side of Gentilly. Ms. Cora and her son lived in their house for thirty years. It is the home where Ms. Cora grew up. Before the storm she was an active member of her community, attending the church where her uncle is pastor in the Ninth Ward, and being a neighborhood mom. That world disappeared when her block was flooded with six feet of water.

Ms. Cora moved from shelter to shelter for a year and a half praying for a way to come home. In January 2007 she finally made it to her empty block where she found her house full of waterlogged possessions. Our volunteers gutted her house, but all she could do was pray for a solution to rebuilding. Her Road Home grant was not forthcoming, and so she continued to wait.

When Katie Mears and her team offered to help Ms. Cora rebuild she refused at first, saying she was sure God would send her Road Home money soon. She told Katie the church should help people who needed assistance more than she. But after waiting and praying, waiting and praying, it finally came to her in prayer that maybe we were the help she had been praying for. She finally agreed to let us help her rebuild on the condition that when the Road Home money does come through, we will allow her to repay us so that someone else can have their house rebuilt too.

We arrange for subcontractors to do mold remediation, electrical wiring, and plumbing. Then volunteers from Polick, Virginia come in and put up sheetrock, paint, lay floors, install trim, doors, and cabinets. Ms. Cora guides us through the process, choosing her own colors and making her house a home. She can't believe it when she sees the new window in her bedroom. Until last week it was still covered in plywood, hiding the broken pane through which her son was rescued from the floodwaters nearly two years ago. We are willing and able to do this work on a relatively small scale, but once again, this is not what the federal government intended when it allocated $11 billion to the Road Home program. The incompetence of ICF is seriously slowing the recovery and creating an enormous amount of pain.

And so the organizer network that we built in the diaspora during the registration drive for the America*Speaks* Community Congress goes into action again. We partner with Barbara Major and Bill Rouselle, who have formed an organization called the Louisiana Diaspora Advocacy Partnership to hold press conferences and rallies. The goal is to force an appeal system that will bring ICF representatives into churches to work with homeowners to resolve their problems.

On the day of the march in Baton Rouge, hoards of homeowners begin to make their way to the steps of the state capitol. One is Charles Jenkins, who, as he has come to say often, now knows what it's like to be "one of those people down there" as the president has unfortunately called us. The fact of the matter is that even the bishop of Louisiana has not received his Road Home check.

Originally it is set that Jenkins will be the main media spokesperson, and he will speak first. But when he arrives he says, "No. We were not the lead organizers of this. I will speak at the end. Someone else should be the one to do the interviews with the press." Shakoor thinks to himself, "You ought to know this by now." He goes back once again to the organizers and says, "No, the bishop doesn't want all that stuff."

Instead, Jenkins moves among crowd. He wants to talk to the people. Shakoor says, "He was like a kid at Christmas that day—talking to everybody, and eventually giving his speech. But he absolutely refused to be given any special status."

The bishop, gracious as always, says he was emulating Shakoor. "The day we participated in the march in Baton Rouge about housing and the right to return, I watched Shakoor's quiet behind-the-scenes capacity to give people hope, to give people voice, and his capacity to listen. Even if the speaker at the microphone may not be honoring the presence of the eighty-five-year-old woman who rode on a bus from Houston, she can walk to Shakoor and suddenly she is the most important person at the rally. Or this youngster, who may have a lot of different agendas—kind of puts people off—and he comes to Shakoor and suddenly that kid has a place."

From his sightline Shakoor says, "The bishop was very clear that we have to be in the moment with people and we have to show them we side with them, and that it is genuine. We're not coming in to speak and then split, or grab a couple of minutes of fame or look for the press. When other powerful religious leaders are doing just the opposite, to see a powerful white religious leader who doesn't try to grab attention and is willing to support unpopular issues—seeing that is what is winning Jenkins so much respect."

Shakoor has done faith-based work for over twenty years but up till now he has treated it as a tactical alliance. "It was never as if I was willing to become a part of any church." Now Shakoor declares something that gives us all great joy. He announces that on Easter this lifelong Muslim, beaten by his teachers for not being Christian, has decided he would like Bishop Jenkins to baptize him into the Christian faith.

He tells me, "I knew early on that this time working with the church was going to be different. I knew it because of Bishop Jenkins. Some of it was this place, which makes you need to have some practice of faith to be able to keep going. But I've grown to feel that the bishop is just this incredible person. There is a humility to him that I really respect. Not studied. Not fake. People are beginning to call him the white Tutu.

"I also admire his attitude toward learning. Someone who came from a more conservative perspective who has been eating up everything he could, increasing his understanding of issues he probably had never looked at before. It is interesting to watch how he can start out knowing very little and inhale new knowledge in a very short period of time. He listens and learns from all. So that's a model I respect.

"I think the world of him. I'd die for him. I think he is one of the most important leaders I've ever met."

The night of the Great Easter Vigil arrives, the night of Shakoor's baptism. The cathedral service begins in darkness as we prepare to hear the great story of salvation history. Shakoor is sitting with his sponsor for baptism, Rosanne Adderly from St. Luke's and two rows of St. Luke's parishioners who have come to support him.

The only light in the cathedral is the Pascal candle, illuminated. We sing the chant, "The Light of Christ. Thanks be to God," three times as the huge candle is carried from the rear to the front of the cathedral's nave.

Then we begin with a series of nine scriptural readings, each one followed by a psalm and a prayer. I am struck by the fact that the focus of each touches upon the spiritual themes that are guiding us in that long journey Karen Armstrong described, away from selfishness and greed and toward greater and greater compassion.

We begin with the story of creation when God gives everything that is to us, above all our humanity. And we pray, "O God, who wonderfully created, and yet more wonderfully restored, the dignity of human nature: Grant that we may share the divine life of him who humbled himself to share our humanity, your Son Jesus Christ our Lord. *Amen.*"

We read the story of Israel's deliverance at the Red Sea, and pray, "O God, whose wonderful deeds of old shine forth even to our own day, you once delivered by the power of your mighty army your chosen people from slavery under Pharaoh, to be a sign for us of the salvation of all nations by the waters of Baptism: Grant that all the peoples of the earth may be numbered among the offspring of Abraham, and rejoice in the inheritance of Israel; through Jesus Christ our Lord. *Amen.*

We pray for the "joy of that heavenly Jerusalem, where all tears are wiped away," a phrase drawn from the bishop's guiding passage for us in our mission from the twenty-first chapter of the Revelation of St. John. We hear two passages from the prophet Ezekiel: "A new heart I will give you, and a new spirit I will put within you; and I will remove from your body the heart of stone and give you a heart of flesh." The second passage is the story of the valley of dry bones when the Lord says to Ezekiel, "Can these dry bones live?" And the prophet answers, "O Lord God, you know." And God says, "Prophesy mortal . . . and breathe upon these slain, that they may live." And the bones come to life, and stand upon their feet, a vast multitude.

Finally we pray my favorite prayer in our whole tradition:

O God of unchangeable power and eternal light: Look favorably upon your whole Church, that wonderful and sacred mystery; by the effectual working of your providence, carry out in tranquility the plan of salvation; let the whole world see and know that things cast down are being raised up, and things which had grown old are being made new, and that all things are being brought to their perfection by him through whom all things were made, your Son Jesus Christ our Lord. *Amen.*

It is now time for the bishop to preach his Easter sermon. Jenkins moves to the pulpit and begins. "It is a special joy for me tonight to welcome into the household of faith my brother Shakoor. I was praying about this today, and I thought, Shakoor, if it were not an imperialist thing to do, I would give you the Greek name of Barnabas, which means 'son of encouragement.' It was Barnabas who gave encouragement to the apostle Paul, after his conversion on the Damascus Road, when Saul ceased his persecution and turned to new life in Jesus Christ."

At the time that Shakoor kneels in front of the bishop and the bishop places his hand on Shakoor's head, marking on his forehead the sign of the cross and saying, "Shakoor, you are sealed by the Holy Spirit in baptism and marked as Christ's own forever," he adds in a whisper, "You are my brother." I can see that the newly baptized is drowned in tears.

Ellene and I have spent days creating Shakoor's present—a shadow box with an illuminated prayer by St. Ignatius Loyola, surrounded by a pattern of beads, shells, and feathers with a distinctly African flavor. The prayer reads:

> Teach us, Good Lord
> To give
> And not to count the cost;
> To fight
> And not to heed the wounds;
> To toil
> And not to seek for rest;
> To labor
> And not to ask for any reward
> Save that of knowing that we do thy will.

After a celebratory dinner, we pull out my Bible and look up all the references to Barnabas in the book of Acts. Shakoor seems like he is in a daze. "That was kind of overwhelming. I thought it was an important step going into Christ's church but his words—it was kind of embarrassing for me. I feel like I'm the prodigal son. I'm not used to that much attention."

I have my own hunches on the significance of Barnabas. The new apostle Paul is thought of as a persecutor of the Christian people. Suddenly, he is called by Christ and the scales fall from his eyes. When no one trusts Saul's sudden conversion, Barnabas is the one who does. And he vouches for Paul before anyone else quite believes the old Saul could be the new Paul, could really be sincere.

I ask Bishop Jenkins what led him to that name. "Shakoor is an encouragement!" The bishop was evidently thinking particularly about the way Shakoor was held at gunpoint after the storm. "He is an encouragement in his very being. Here is a guy who had no stake in New Orleans. He came here immediately and was drawn down upon by mercenaries with violence. He should have left and never returned, but he didn't. He stayed. And of course Barnabas was an encouragement to St. Paul. That's what I see him doing in a way that does not call attention to himself. He is very sacrificial in the life he leads. He certainly isn't perfect. None of us are. But I find in his quiet respect for the dignity of all, and his quiet belief in the New Jerusalem, and his capacity to be present to so many different kinds of people, he's an encouragement to me. His willingness to sacrifice for the betterment of the community—there's a great example there."

## CHAPTER 10

# THE NEW JERUSALEM

SHORTLY AFTER EASTER WE RECEIVE AN EXCITING PIECE OF NEWS. THE bishops of our church from every corner of our country have agreed to hold their next national gathering in New Orleans. Even the Archbishop of Canterbury, my old friend Rowan Williams, will be coming all the way from London to join us.

We will be hosting hundreds, and it will fall to us to frame what they see and feel. If the bishop's moment, when he was thrown back by Carolyn Lukensmeyer's message, "This is not wholly about New Orleans, but about all of us in America" is indicative of something terribly important, then this national encounter shortly after the anniversary may be critical.

It is summertime and high season for volunteers and interns coming from everywhere to participate in the resurrection of the city. One is Pam Rapcienski, a passionate devotee of New Orleans finishing a political science major at Fordham University in the Bronx. With Pam's assistance, we will spend the summer crafting a document that tells visitors everything you ever wanted to know about the state of the New Orleans recovery.

Pam's passion for what our work means is representative of tens of thousands of twenty-something-year-olds still flocking to the city. It is as if the city has been adopted as the cause of a generation. So inspired are these youth by a possibility they see for building a new kind of

American city that is founded on a fundamentally new approach to our racial history that many say they would easily devote a lifetime to bringing the new community to birth.

Pam is burning up the Internet. She and my brother, Simon, who drives down from Atlanta frequently, pair up with Shakoor and two remarkable young women from Common Ground, Gabe Barry and Casey Leigh. Gabe and Casey are now interning for the diocese and creating a bi-weekly electronic e-newsletter that goes out to thousands called *In the N.O.* Thanks to Joe Goldman at America*Speaks,* we are given a small grant to work with some techies to create some innovative social networking possibilities. Our team begins to post on blogs, build web pages, upload flash movies on YouTube, and generally explore how to build a major social network of peers who share a vision for the future possibilities of this culturally unique city.

While there are many positive and hopeful dynamics in the recovery, there are also huge challenges. We begin our report with an overview of the case management system. It is funded through Homeland Security and FEMA by a donation made to this country at the time of the storm from the Kingdom of Quatar to the tune of $66 million. So far no federal tax dollars have been allocated to assist Katrina survivors with their long-term recovery plan, only funds that came from overseas. The faith-based agencies that have been providing case management since September 2005 have raised another $70 million in private donations to further this work. Collectively the Katrina Aid Today consortium of nine national partners has so far helped 164,000 displaced individuals in thirty-two states, begin to help themselves.

We have also begun to refurbish homes. Each of our homeowners receives an average of $9,158 in material supplies and an average of $3,000 in volunteer labor. We also provide hundreds of dollars' worth of direct services and donated goods, furniture, and appliances. So far our church has gutted 875 homes at an estimated value of $5.28 million. We have recently begun, in the summer of 2007, to refurbish homes. Nearly 175,000 people have received free food and supplies through our mobile unit ministries, manned by volunteers, and the work of these ministries in the Ninth Ward has led to the community in that neighborhood founding a new Episcopal mission called All Souls. The St. George's café, which serves a growing population of homeless folks unable to find affordable housing, and the Mobile Loaves and Fishes vehicle operated by Trinity Church, have together reached 53,475 residents of the city. We also have a mobile medical unit operated by St. Anna's that has served 5,948 patients, and we support the St. Thomas Clinic, the first medical facility for the uninsured to open following the storm.

The Jericho Road Housing Initiative has begun to develop attractive, affordable homes for purchase in Central City. We are developing fifty-five homes in the first phase of our efforts, cleaning and redeveloping an industrial brown field in the heart of Central City that will provide an entire city block for the development of housing, small businesses, and supportive services—a mix to be determined by residents. We are purchasing our first property for the development of low-cost rental units in the neighborhood as well. New two-bedroom homes are priced at $120,000 with up to $75,000 in subsidies available to qualified buyers. Our Homecoming Center at St. Paul's Church in Lakeview, run by an outstanding resident leader named Connie Uddo, has served 10,656 residents with an array of support and services to help families who have made it back to the city stabilize their lives.

We obviously want the bishops, the press, and the politicians coming our way to understand the scale of the work—how many have and continue to come together to stand with us, the poor, fighting for the right to return home with dignity. And yet we are but one denomination. According to the National Council of Churches, 1.1 million Americans have volunteered in the Gulf Coast recovery since the storm.

One thing it seems very important for the country to comprehend is who so many Americans have proven to be. The volunteers who have driven the progress of this recovery have not sacrificed for the "safe" above-sea-level neighborhoods or the economically secure residents of the city. Volunteers are still coming in larger numbers than ever to help heal the lives of the same vulnerable Americans we saw trapped, suffering, and dying on our televisions in August 2005, and our neighbors in communities like Lakeview and Broadmoor, which were both heavily flooded.

This is what I want the president and visitors at the time of the anniversary to ask themselves: What is it that millions of Americans are saying when they come to gut and rebuild this city block by block with their own bare hands? What does it mean when millions sacrifice personally to finance the purchase of building materials for residents who have yet to receive their Road Home money from the government? Will our visitors hear what young people are saying by the hundreds when they come to serve the children of the city as teachers in our struggling schools? I hear millions of Americans saying they love their neighbor as themselves and want those beliefs and values reflected in our public policy. When you stand inside the recovery you can feel the pulse of America beating strongly.

This is heartening because we have some serious reforms to accomplish. As huge as the response by incredibly decent, caring citizens has been, we have not yet made our impact and values as a nation felt in some critical areas.

At the time of the storm FEMA moved 90,406 Louisiana families into what was termed "temporary units." These are travel trailers that provide 320 square feet of living space. According to Tracie Washington, a civil rights attorney who heads the Louisiana Justice Institute, in the summer of 2008, 86,000 families are still housed in these travel trailers throughout the Gulf Coast, and 30,723 of these households are in Louisiana. Families have not received adequate, or oftentimes any, funding from the $11 billion Road Home program to rebuild their dwellings, so they continue to live in inhumane spaces.

The majority of trailers are parked in front of still uninhabitable homes, 3,479 families live in their trailers located in commercial parks, and another 2,237 live in group-sites surrounded by barbed wire, patrolled by armed guards employed by Blackwater, and located in remote sections of the state not serviced by public transportation.

According to the Louisiana Housing Finance Agency, 105,155 affordable homes, rental and owned, or 51.4 percent of housing in New Orleans was severely damaged in the storm. The agency estimates the current demand for rental units that are affordable to low- and moderate-income households in New Orleans falls somewhere between 29,000 and 50,000 units. The demand for homes to purchase, affordable to low- and moderate-income households is between 20,000 and 40,000 units.

The effect of this housing shortage has been to drive housing costs in New Orleans through the roof. A chart published by LHFA entitled "Housing Affordability Mismatch" shows a single-family home in a low-income neighborhood rents for an average of $1,500 per month. A two-bedroom apartment in the same neighborhood on average, rents for $1,000 per month, and a studio an average of $800 per month. But salaries of police and sheriffs average $600 per week, of bank tellers $500 per week, of cashiers about $400 per week, and of housekeepers about $300 per week.

With a limited supply of housing and a sharp increase in prices, homelessness in New Orleans has increased 400 percent and is now six times the national average. The homeless population has reached unprecedented levels for a U.S. city: one in every twenty-five residents of the city of New Orleans is homeless according to *USA Today*.

Obviously, ICF, the administrator of the Road Home program, has a role to play in efficiently and effectively channeling allocated funding to applicants waiting to rebuild their homes. Through its small-rental program, ICF is also supposed to be channeling funding to small landlords to repair affordable rental properties and make them available quickly, but their procedure requires landlords to buy materials and make repairs first, then be reimbursed. Many small landlords have not been able to raise the capital or qualify for bank loans to make this possible.

The glue in this process to move a displaced resident into housing and on a recovery track is case management, because it is that force of trained workers that can link people to available affordable housing and put together the resources that can provide apartment deposits, pay to hire a moving van, and provide some basic furniture and appliances. FEMA is scheduled to end case management for all Katrina survivors in March 2009, and the scope of case management is being drastically reduced in March 2008.

HUD has taken several steps to remove thousands of public housing units from the market in New Orleans, as part of a larger national policy to demolish public housing complexes throughout the country in favor of contracting with for-profit developers to create mixed-income housing. This policy, known as HOPE VI, reduces the number of very affordable units and invests taxpayer dollars to create larger numbers of market-rate units that turn profits for the developers building them.

At the time of the storm, public housing residents living in 1950s, garden style, historically landmarked public housing, situated on valuable in town tracts of land that were not flooded, were forcibly evacuated leaving all their property and belongings behind. These complexes were then surrounded by barbed wire fences, and security door and window covers were installed at a considerable cost to prevent re-entry. A policy to demolish public housing was established that leaves a few hundred units standing: 1,841 units will be replaced over the next few years, only 744 of which will be available at deep affordability. This is a net loss of over 2,764 units of affordable housing. Only 744 units out of 5,146 are guaranteed for New Orleans's poorest citizens.

The secretary of HUD, Alphonso Jackson, is under investigation by the FBI. And this is the agency that will assume responsibility from FEMA for housing and relocating families still living in FEMA trailers under a program called DHAP. While one branch of HUD is moving ahead to destroy housing units that could be rehabilitated, at least temporarily for the purpose of improved emergency housing, another arm of the same agency is searching for a plan to relocate and house the nearly 31,000 families in Louisiana in FEMA trailers.

Those of us who are carrying the responsibility for case management are beginning to receive appeals to come to HUD and FEMA's rescue by helping with the trailer relocation process. But FEMA is also ending funding for case management on March 1, 2008, and HUD remains determined to destroy available public housing units at precisely the same time. All of this in the face of recent reports from the Centers for Disease Control and Prevention that families in FEMA trailers are being poisoned by carcinogenic formaldehyde fumes released from the building materials used to make the travel trailers FEMA purchased.

As I am working on this report, I realize statistics only convey part of the picture. I am glad the Episcopal bishops, and the press, and our elected leaders will be traveling through the community. I want them to have at least one of the gut-wrenching moments I have every hour of every day. I want them to feel what it is like to be driving the kids to an outing and hear one adorable boy innocently say, as we drive past the clusters of tents springing up under the interstate, "that's where my family lives."

If they were to travel into the hinterlands of the state, they would meet individuals like Ray and Laura Ann. Ray, who lives in a travel trailer in the euphemistically named "Renaissance Village," used to be a chef at the well-known and much beloved New Orleans institution Mandina's, but the storm completely wiped him out. The best he's been able to do since the storm is to find short-order jobs at IHOP and Waffle House. As he puts it, "Those pennies don't go nowhere." His family has not been able to qualify for food stamps. At times they literally do not have food to eat.

He and his children have been living in one of the four hundred tiny Baker trailers in Renaissance Park for nearly two years. Ray is a powerhouse. But you can tell he is becoming desperate in a situation where there is seemingly no way out. For a minute he gives voice to an inner tape that must run through his mind continuously, "I didn't ask to be this way. I didn't ask to come here period. I have got to get them kids out of this place. Why did I let this happen?" Then he snaps out of victim mode, and his whole being swells before our eyes. "I got to be the man that I am. I have to stand up to the fact that I'm a man still yet! Regardless of the situation. Regardless of how they look at me. Regardless of how they think about me. I am still a man. And if I want it, I got to stand up to the pain. I got to somehow make that move."

He looks up. "I'm stepping out on faith, because guess what? I have nuttin! I have zero! I have ze-ro! Nuttin. I have to ask people for the things I need. I don't have a bed for those kids. I don't even have an ice box."

Ray takes us over to meet the widow of his best friend. Her name is Laura Ann. Laura is living on her own with three children and one grandchild. They are all having terrible health problems since living in this trailer.

"I just found out my youngest son is sufferin' with seizures and asthma. My other son is sufferin' with seizures. I have a daughter with seizures and asthma. I am sufferin' with cancer. I want to move out of here but the rent out there is too high. Once I pay the rent I'd have no money for food and clothes for my kids. I'd have to get furniture for us to lay down on the bed. I really need help and I am tryin' my hardest. I'm goin' back to school, tryin' to get my GED, for me and my kids to better my life, so I can help my kids better their life. I need somebody who gonna say, 'Lean on me.' I don't have nobody I can lean on right now. Nobody."

I think to myself, "A case manager would be somebody, but there aren't enough to go around. And the government is about to close the program down. It's insane."

Pam has convinced me it is time to reach out to her cousin Barbara in Washington at the law firm of Krivit and Krivit. By the time the Krivits arrive in New Orleans it is clear that the closure of case management for all survivors of Katrina is the number one crisis we must tackle.

Immediately after signing the contract with them, and digging in on this challenge, we learn that Katrina Aid Today has received word that the Department of Health and Human Services (DHHS) has issued a closed request for proposals for future disaster case management that precludes national voluntary agencies such as ours, who have been providing this sort of case management in the aftermath of catastrophes since the 1950s. Instead, competition has been limited by DHHS to private for-profit contractors. And there are disturbing, unconfirmed reports from sources inside FEMA that the company expected to receive the contract is ICF, the firm that has completely botched the failed Road Home program and has been sanctioned by the Louisiana state legislature.

I learn that these trends we seem to be seeing out of Washington at HUD, at DHHS, and Homeland Security/FEMA, to name a few, have been given a name by a writer named Naomi Klein. When I begin to turn the pages of Klein's book *The Shock Doctrine*, I can't believe my eyes. It's as though she is describing my life.

Klein writes about several examples of major no-bid federal contracts going to for-profit companies immediately after Katrina, and describes the Louisiana State Legislature "crawling with corporate lobbyists helping to lock in those big opportunities: lower taxes, fewer regulations, cheaper workers, and a 'smaller, safer city'—which meant plans to level the public housing projects and replace them with condos. . . . I call these orchestrated raids on the public sphere in the wake of catastrophic events, combined with the treatment of disasters as exciting market opportunities, 'disaster capitalism.'" So, I discover, a term has been coined for this incredibly disturbing dynamic we keep confronting.

Of all the politicians and celebrities who arrive for the anniversary, there is one who wants to hear a report on what our concerns are with Washington and the federal government. It is Senator Barack Obama, who has scheduled a small meeting with grassroots leaders through All Congregations Together, at Mary Queen of Vietnam Catholic Church in New Orleans East. The morning of the meeting, Bishop Jenkins, Shakoor, and I head for the church full of expectation. The bishop has decided he is going to share publicly for the first time our concern that ICF is favored to receive the all-important contract for designing future disaster case management.

We arrive at the huge Catholic Church with three thousand Vietnamese members and find our way to a modest Sunday school classroom. On a blackboard scrawled in white chalk is a message welcoming "Senator Barack Obama Community Organizer." The senator arrives with so little fanfare I don't even realize he has entered the room until he's greeted half the people in it. He is wearing an off-white button-down shirt, and some gray slacks. As he moves to sit in one of the desks at the front of the room he casually rolls up his sleeves.

Mary Fontenot, lead organizer of ACT, welcomes Obama. Then the senator begins by saying he is here not to give a speech but to listen and learn from us. His opening remarks are the most succinct and accurate summary of the main issues we face I have heard any politician give since I arrived in the city. I'm impressed. The bishop, true to form, holds back his comments for quite some time, until most of the people in the room have a chance to speak.

Then Jenkins takes the floor. When the bishop says that federal funding for case management is in danger of going to ICF, the company administering the Road Home program, every person in the room gasps. One woman actually lets out a scream. The bishop continues, "The way DHHS has handled the bidding for this contract follows an alarming pattern that is being investigated by Congress. It was a closed, no-bid request for proposals to six for-profit companies." The bishop continues. "I am thankful to Barbara Zientek and the good work of Krivit and Krivit on behalf of the poor. Case management both gives fish to the hungry and teaches the hungry to fish. It is a program of helping people stand on their own. The Congressional bog frustrates me because it is not one political party or another that pays the price for this—the price is paid by those who struggle to stand on their own and rebuild their lives." I can see the senator nodding vigorously.

"Religious and nonprofit groups have not enriched themselves with case management work; in fact, we have raised and given away more money than we were given by the government. Even so, case management may become a for-profit exercise. I do not understand the expansion of what the writer Naomi Klein calls 'disaster capitalism' in what is supposed to be a season of faith-based initiative.

"There is a moral issue that as a Christian I must address. As Christians, we do not see humans as a means to an end, especially if the end is profit. This is particularly offensive when we see the poor or the traumatized as a means to an end. As Christians we see humans as an end in ourselves. As John Henry Newman wrote, and I must paraphrase, *it is the cross that places due value upon everything*. The cross of Jesus Christ, the hope of Christ crucified and resurrected, gives value to all."

Finally September 22 comes and the day of the great gathering of bishops. As Rowan emerges from the plane, my heart is in my throat. It means so much to me that he, of all people, has come. Williams shakes the hand of the bishop first, and all the others in our group, then comes over to me last. After giving me a warm hug, he whispers in my ear in a tone of deep concern, "Oh my dear, are you *okay?*"

The deep compassion in his heart washes over me like a balm. It feels like that moment on 9/11 when he prayed, "We are free to bring our fear before God." It is like he is saying, "You know you could admit it to me if you're not okay and that would be alright." We don't often give ourselves permission to go to that place in the course of this work, but wise, gentle Rowan, true to form, starts there. The archbishop pulls back to an arm's length and appraises the look in my eye with that expression that says, "Tell me the truth." "Yes," I nod, "I am okay. It's hard, but I'm okay. I really am." Just knowing he will see what we are living through with his own eyes makes me feel stronger.

A crazy week begins. Over one hundred members of the press corps are in town and a furious pace of activities are scheduled. But it is a week of that immense joy that is found in the midst of sorrow when hundreds care enough to stand with you. The first big event is the dedication of All Souls, our new mission in the Lower Ninth Ward. Shakoor and Vickie round up all the children, and as I have asked, spend some time with them teaching them about who the Archbishop of Canterbury is. I've suggested that they be encouraged to think of a burning question they would like to ask a very wise and holy man and am in suspense to discover what that question will prove to be.

While they are doing that, I am hastily putting finishing touches on a group document being circulated in the House of Bishops as a draft for resolution to the U.S. Congress. The document draws on statements already ratified by the Episcopal House of Bishops on March 21, 2006, the International Day for the Elimination of Racial Discrimination, in which the bishops state as a body their belief that the catastrophes that occurred in the Gulf Coast in 2005 were dramatic evidence of the continuing sin of racism in this country. In it the bishops provide a succinct theological argument for why racism is a sin.

> The Christian doctrine of humanity holds that all are made in the image of God. It is in our diversity that we discover the fullness of that image. If we judge one class or race or gender better than another, we violate that desire and intent of God. And when our social and cultural systems exacerbate or codify such judgments, we do violence to that which God has made. . . . When Jesus entered the synagogue in his first

act of public ministry (Luke 4), he read from the prophet Isaiah. The vision he proclaimed is known as the desire of God, the peaceable kingdom, a society of justice and shalom, or the city set on a hill. It is an icon of what God intends for all creation: that human beings live in justice and peace with one another, that the poor are fed and housed and clothed, the ill are healed, prisoners set free, and that the whole created order is restored to right relationship. That vision is our goal and vocation as Christians.

In the new document the bishops will add:

> This nation has a long history of struggle for racial justice. . . . Today that struggle continues in the form of the Gulf Coast recovery. During our visit to New Orleans the bishops have witnessed powerful signs of God's presence in this struggle. Over 1.1 million citizens of our country have worked with unprecedented fervor to cherish and restore the many lives violated before, during, and since the flood. Greater leadership at the national level in this moment could broaden this sustained American commitment into a movement that would make history.

I ride to the big event at All Souls with Canon Scott Albergate, our Canon for Mission, and Jim Rosenthal and Tim Livesey of the Archbishop's Lambeth Palace staff. We leave the Intercontinental Hotel downtown, accompanied by police escort, and race through the streets still littered with devastated homes. When we arrive there is a crowd of paparazzi who ambush Archbishop Rowan and Bishop Jenkins the minute they emerge from the car. Fr. Shola, the priest in charge of the new mission, welcomes all from a podium set up in the parking lot, then Jenkins and Williams make brief statements.

The archbishop begins in a deeply pastoral tone, empathizing with those gathered as people who have struggled with feelings of betrayal, abandonment, and terrifying vulnerability. "But the church is here," Williams reminds us all, "to be with you. The church will not abandon you, as God does not abandon us—ever. That is part of what it means to be the church—to love our neighbor as God loves us and to be a sign of that love."

Jenkins uses the opportunity to reinforce the fact that the church is here to care, but we are also here to fight for justice. He informs the press and the public of the same issues and data we have shared with Senator Obama. Then our silver-haired, horn-rim-be-spectacled bishop winds up with stirring references to the sixty thousand anti-racism protesters from cities and towns throughout America who are at this moment marching in Jena, Louisiana: our dear colleagues Gabe Barry, Casey Leigh, Tracie Washington, Joe Blakk, Jerome Smith, Mary Fontenot, and many others included among them. Jenkins concludes with the thrust of the black power sign. The crowd erupts in cheers and applause.

The bishops' move from the podium to tour the new mission sparks a paparazzi frenzy. About a hundred photographers and cameramen literally chase them around the property. Our kids, who have arrived with Shakoor and Vickie in a state of excitement over this unusual occasion, think it's fabulous fun. Princess grabs my hand, and in one big mass we all race around following the archbishop and the bishop, and the maniacal journalistic stampede. The children are squealing with delight. I think it is utterly absurd. Finally, once the media are satisfied that they've gotten the shots they need, the frenzy begins to subside. As Archbishop Rowan gathers with the children, I have the chance to introduce each one by name. I begin with the little girl clutching my hand.

"Your Grace, may I present Princess."

Williams looks bewildered for a moment, then lowers his eyes to register the fact that Princess is a nine-year-old African American girl with pigtails, who looks back at him with big doe-shaped eyes and says, "Hi." Now I get to hear what the children have decided their burning question for the great holy man should be. Cha'von is their chosen spokesperson.

"We was wonderin' with what all's happenin' up in Jena, you know, with the nooses and all that—'cause it makes us real sad—why do people do that? Why can't everybody just get along?"

The faces of the children are somber with hurt but their eyes sparkle with anticipation as they wait for a word of wisdom that will help them understand. Inside I am so proud that they have really given this thought and searched their hearts for a question worthy of the moment. They could not have asked a better one.

We huddle close together locked in concentration. For a minute I am worried that Rowan, being from overseas, will not know enough about what has transpired in Jena and why sixty thousand people have gathered in the small upstate rural town. They are there to show their solidarity with the African American youth who have been charged with second-degree manslaughter and assault with a deadly tennis shoe. But evidently the archbishop does know because he acknowledges the hanging of the nooses on the playground where the Jena Six attended school, and their incarceration—mere boys. Then Rowan speaks. In essence he says, "People do these things out of fear, and if we want to stop these terrible racial acts we must find a way for people to begin to feel safe with one another." It sounds simple, but in fact his response is profound.

The children just love Rowan. They bond with him immediately. Shakoor lets the archbishop know quietly that Princess's mother died four days ago of AIDS. The priest takes a moment with her and asks, "Are you feeling very sad?" Princess says, "Yes, but I decided I could feel sad by myself at home while everyone was here, or I could feel sad with everyone around me. And I decided to come." Again, my heart swells. It only takes a few moments to appreciate the maturity and resilience of these children.

After the dedication I have to go immediately to the convention center to help with the preparations for the huge ecumenical service about to ensue. Shakoor calls me on his cell to say, "You can't imagine how ecstatic the kids are. They can't stop talking about how special the archbishop made them feel, and they are furiously debating how to follow his advice—how they can reach out to help white folks who fear them feel befriended and safe. It's really incredible. I wish you could hear this conversation. By the way, they want to go to London and visit him at the palace." Wow! I think to myself, what an incredible experience it would be to be able to do that with our dear ones.

An hour later the kids have arrived at the convention center, and thousands have taken their seats. The service begins with a rousing version of "Christ is made the sure foundation," led by a huge interracial gospel choir named Shades of Praise. I look around and see a family gathered that would never have existed before the storm. All our partners who aren't in Jena are here. I see Saundra, Raynard, Gus and his wife, Kathryn, Nell, and many, many more.

Every faith group in the city is represented on the stage. Every Episcopal bishop in the country is in the house. On the side of the stage opposite Shades of Praise are Irvin Mayfield and his quartet. Giant flat screens suspended from the ceiling of the hall show images of the millions of Americans who have come to stand with us engaged in acts of friendship and mercy. The theme of the service, gleaned from the archbishop's tremendous book *Resurrection,* is "Humanity Renewed, Restored, Re-centered in God."

True to form Charles Jenkins begins his opening remarks with a bit of self-deprecating humor. He welcomes the 104th Archbishop of Canterbury, "and to put that in perspective," Jenkins adds, "I am the 10th Bishop of Louisiana." The whole room laughs. Then Bishop Jenkins acknowledges a factor of Rowan's visit that has frustrated the two of us to no end. He says, "I want you all to know, that the archbishop's schedule is so heavy that he is not even going to have the opportunity to eat a single fine meal in New Orleans, but only that hotel food." The whole crowd spontaneously boos. That is a Louisianian's definition of hell.

The serious note of Bishop's Jenkins' remarks is one of deep sincere gratitude. "All that we have done has been possible because we have had the strength of the entire Church behind us. Communities of faith are rebuilding this city and we are grateful for all you have done to help."

The invocation is prayed by the great African American Baptist pastor Bishop J. Douglas Wiley, and then we hear the Old Testament lesson from Zechariah 8:3–13.

> Thus says the LORD of hosts: Old men and old women shall again sit in the streets of Jerusalem, each with staff in hand because of their great age. And the streets of the city will be full of boys and girls playing in its streets. Thus says the LORD of hosts: Even though it seems impossible to the remnant of the people in these days, should it be impossible to me, says the LORD of hosts? Thus says the LORD of hosts: I will save my people from the east country and from the west country; and I will bring them to live in Jerusalem. They shall be my people and I will be their God, in faithfulness and righteousness. Thus says the LORD of hosts: Let your hands be strong.

Before the archbishop's address there is a thunderous rendition of "In Christ there is no East or West, in him no South or North, but one great fellowship of love throughout the whole wide earth." The New Testament lesson is a familiar one, Matthew 25:34–40, which ends, "Truly I tell you, just as you did it to one of the least of these who are members of my family, you did it unto me."

The archbishop weaves the two lessons together beautifully, preaching in essence about what we call by the Greek name *koinonia*: the ideal state of fellowship and community that God intends for us. It is in *koinonia*, in communion, that what makes us persons is understood. Without one another we cannot experience what we are made for. "Like a glowing coal," Desmond Tutu writes, "that loses its heat, and more significantly, its ability to provide warmth when it is separated from other coals and when it is forced to exist on its own away from the hearth," so human beings lose our heat, our ability to glow and warm others, when we are separated and isolated from one another. Archbishop Rowan, very much in this vein, begins:

> Every city, every community at one point or another has to ask itself, "What do we owe one another?" People speak, don't they, about the contract between people and government and they notice when it's not there. People speak of the recognition of dignity owed to one another. About the respect that we owe to one another. But I wonder if we are not missing something? When I say to a friend, "I owe you one," it's a way of saying thank you. And perhaps the bottom line is that what we owe to one another most deeply of all is gratitude. We are indebted to one another. I am indebted to you for your existence because I would not be myself without you. And a society, a community, a city that can get to that level of recognition is one that lives from a deeper place than one that simply talks about contract or even respect.

> And the gospel reading opens up that further and deeper dimension which says that what we owe one another is exactly what we owe to Jesus Christ. Jesus Christ who gives us life, who gives us our very being, the Word from whom all things were made and has become one flesh with us. Jesus Christ has given us a new creation—the humanity renewed, restored, and re-centered that we are celebrating tonight. Jesus Christ who gives us hope, who gives us the capacity to move away from our fears, who gives us strength and joy. We owe Christ big time, as they say. And the gospel tells us that it's that level of owing, that level of indebtedness that we have to try to introduce into our relations with one another. Because the Stranger who waits for us, especially in the stranger, in the naked, in the sick, in the imprisoned, waits for us with a gift of life given within them. Without them we will not live. And that of course is why in this city at the moment absences are so painful.

> And that gets me back to the first reading of this evening. . . . What makes a great and Godly city is that it's a safe place for old people to sit and children to play in the streets. The children who have time to play and the old who have time to sit. There are many forces in our modern society which would quite like to see them relegated out of sight. But they are the ones who remind us what we're here for as

human beings—for gratitude, for joy. Let us pray to see again the streets of the city full of boys and girls playing.

When Irvin Mayfield and the older jazz greats follow the sermon with an incredible twenty-minute improvisational version of "When the Saints Go Marching In," it is as if the auditorium erupts in an enacted version of the sermon the archbishop just gave. Our children from Treme, Princess in the lead, rush from their seats and start the dance. Thousands fall into line behind them. Everyone from Little T who is nine, to Gus Newport who is seventy-two, and everyone in between. Every time the kids pass the stage they wave and sing out to Rowan, their new best buddy, and Rowan waves back. All the bishops in their flowing cassocks are swaying, and Imams and Rabbis are clapping, and I wonder what our British visitors make of it all.

It is at the conclusion of the week that Gus Newport, the former mayor of Berkeley, California, makes his address to the House of Bishops, and the whole body of Episcopal bishops and spouses discuss what is needed from the nation if we are to achieve this unprecedented remaking for which we pray. That discussion must take place in light of the reality that so many of our governmental agencies and institutional structures seem determined to produce the same old outcome, instead of something inspiring and new.

Gus heartily affirms that our move to hire expert assistance in Washington, D.C. is a bold and expensive but absolutely necessary step that we must find funds to sustain. In every sentence he emphasizes the vital importance of innovation and creativity if we are to seize the great moment of opportunity to break from the past.

Newport decries the lack of vision and leadership from government at every level, but praises the leadership of youth. If we are to succeed, the former mayor believes it is going to take some profound restructuring of the body politic, because the game in Washington, Baton Rouge, and in City Hall, is no longer serving the great principles of this nation, which the people hold and are the bedrock of healthy communities. Newport wants to see us organize behind an inspiring vision, with the solid underpinning of a compelling, common philosophy that frames what this work is about, and he ends by calling every bishop, every volunteer, every donor, every caring citizen to create a movement that will undertake this generational work.

## CHAPTER 11

# LIVE LIKE YOU WERE DYING

ONE DAY IN LATE MAY 2008, I AM STRAIGHTENING SOME PAPERS IN MY office and come across a cardboard box in the corner of the room. In it is a curious combination of haphazardly piled documents and artifacts. As I start to dig through them, I have the feeling people must have when they open a time capsule. It is as if, for a minute, I have returned to my old life of poring through musty diaries from the past.

Stacked on top of each other are layers and layers of images and articles from 9/11 and Katrina—now crumpled and yellowed by time—shuffled together in no particular chronological order. In the upper regions of the pile are copies of some of the children's letters that came to us in the chapel in the fall of 2001. Among them is my favorite—Claudia's letter to the firefighter listing all the hair-raising catastrophic ways her young imagination can think of dying.

Since I love that letter so much I pause and read it again. Claudia was certain of one thing—that she would not die in a fire, "Because," she said to the firefighter, "people like you would go into the fire to save an ordinary person like me. And that's what makes you so great, courageous, brave, terrific, wonderful, special people."

Underneath that letter is an article by Dr. Stephen Post, Director of the Institute for Research on Unlimited Love. I see by the date that the piece was written shortly after 9/11. As I glance at the lead for the story I see that Post is relaying an account of a journalist interviewing the famous children's television personality, Mr. Rogers, and asking him on behalf of parents, "What should we say to our children when they ask us questions about 9/11?" Mr. Rogers replied simply, "Tell them to keep their eyes on the helpers."

Digging deeper in the box I find an old color photograph showing one side of the interior of the chapel with thousands of children's letters taped to the walls and the pews—papering every inch. Suddenly I have a sense of all those impressionable young eyes watching us— watching all the helpers. Putting their crayons and pencils to paper they told us what they saw. They saw what makes human beings great.

Beneath those pictures are several more photographs from New Orleans. These are of young ladies in their late teens and early twenties straining to lift crates of debris as they gut a flooded home. What strikes me immediately is how vulnerable the girls look against the grim backdrop of destruction. I think to myself, "Why are so many kids who at their age should be having fun, choosing to shoulder such a heavy responsibility?"

I sit for a moment looking at the images side by side. Then suddenly my mind produces an answer: "These youth in New Orleans are the generation of children who wrote the letters papering the chapel's walls." It is an "Oh my God!" kind of moment.

I am thrown back to something Shakoor said to me when I first met him in early 2006. As he watched the waves of young people pouring into the Lower Ninth Ward coming from across the country into such a forbidding place. Shakoor said he was reminded of the fact that seemingly stagnant periods of our national history can often be deceiving. I remember he put it this way: "When you cannot see it, something else is there dwelling, invisible but gathering strength, preparing to rise up."

After that day my curiosity is piqued, and I begin to do some research. I discover that statistics gathered over the past few years reinforce the observation that an unusually strong altruistic streak is being exhibited by youth who grew up in the shadow of 9/11. It happens that these young people comprise the largest generation in our nation's history. There are 42 million 16 to 25-year-olds who watched the Twin Towers collapse. If the years 1981–2000 are used, as is common in market research, then the size of the Millennial Generation in the United States is approximately 76 million.

According to the Pew Foundation's *Gen Next* survey 83 percent of American Freshmen surveyed in 2005 volunteered at least occasionally during their high school senior year. And 71 percent said they volunteered on a weekly basis. In an Associated Press article posted in April of 2007, studies conducted by the Corporation for National and Community Service show volunteerism at record levels in the years post-9/11, with the volunteer rates among 16 to 29-year-olds almost doubling. The Chief Executive Officer of the Community Service Corporation, David Eisner, is quoted in a report as saying, "Out of the tragedy of 9/11 and the devastation of hurricanes has come an unmistakable good."

The Claudias of our country—a whole generation—are coming of age right now. There is no question that hundreds of thousands of struggling Gulf Coast survivors view the youth who are doing the heavy labor as angels of mercy—exhibiting what makes human beings great. Not only are the Millennials rebuilding homes, but they are also going into the fire of our violent inner city neighborhoods and the ruins of our crumbling schools to save ordinary people like them.

Something of the relentless love exhibited by their heroes who gave their lives at the time of 9/11 has seemingly come alive in them. Now my ears are alert to listening to what they are saying about their motivations. Every day I hear statements like Katie Mears's, describing why she takes on the most difficult Katrina cases when she could be living a conventional twenty-something life: "To me giving up on anybody is not an option." It is exactly what I heard the first-responders say inside the pile.

This is the ethic that is saving New Orleans and may save our country as well. It is a mindset in great contrast to the broken promise of levees that did not hold back the waters of Lake Ponchartrain, as the superb engineering of the Trade Center's "bathtub" held back the Hudson River. It could not be more different than the betrayal of a failed government response that did not deploy anything like the F14's that immediately flew over Manhattan. It is the opposite of the hurt inflicted by a distant President who did not walk the debris laced with corpses in the Lower Nine within days like he walked the smoking pile at the edge of Wall Street.

It is incredibly hopeful to realize that 50 million young Americans of this generation will be eligible to vote in 2008, and that the vast majority of them completely reject the notion that any human life is dispensable. How could they accept such an ethic? This is the 9/11 generation.

What one chooses to do with his or her life is the ultimate high-stakes choice, since we have but one life to live. Sometimes it takes a reminder that our days are not guaranteed to focus our attention on making a conscious decision. With a jolt that jogs our awareness of mortality, we often ask what would it look like (as the country music song says) "to live like you were dying."

I am still grateful for that moment when I thought it was all over because of the way it reoriented my attention. I received a glimpse into the future, a foretaste of what those last few seconds of life might feel like. It's still much harder for me to forget, even seven years later, that ultimately I will die. I am so aware there is a moment when all of this will end, and before it does, there will be that moment when I will apprehend that it is almost over.

It is that instant that concerns me more than the moment of death. I worry much more about the final assessment, "How well and truly did you live your life?" than I do death itself. And although I do believe absolutely, after my experience on 9/11, that my life will be gathered back at that point into the arms of a loving Creator, if I felt I had squandered my life, could I, in that moment of self-assessment, forgive myself?

I think about this question since 9/11: How do I want to feel in that moment? And I know one thing for sure. I want to feel reconciled. I want to feel that I spent my life on what really mattered most as best I could discern it. Faith and experience have helped me learn what some of those things might be.

As we were running from the black cloud that day, it was very telling that our instinct was not entirely for self-protection, but equally to reach out to strangers, frozen in their tracks, to help them keep going. You were a life, and I did not want to see you die. It was surprising in such an extreme moment of life and death to discover how willingly we let go of safety because we valued something else much more. There was no question that we experienced a shared fate, even with total strangers. It wasn't me whose life was on the line, it was us. That experience showed me if I want to feel reconciled in that last moment, to feel I spent my life on what is ultimately important when I look straight at imminent death, I must let go of safety and spend my life on "us."

Inside the darkness of the black debris cloud, and the cloud of shock and grief that enveloped our entire country, it appears something began to happen to many of us on that terrible day. Instead of being permanently shattered, we were by grace dramatically and mysteriously opened to grow and use our lives in generative ways for the life and wellbeing of one another.

In the second darkness—the pain and death of post-Katrina New Orleans—millions more were cracked open by contact with suffering and grief. Again, despite New Orleans's multi-generational destruction, our recent decimation, our floundering elected leadership, and the fear many have of the poverty and pain in our city, we see in the helpers in New Orleans the growing presence of an incredible light.

This light is not only in the young volunteers. I've never known so many people as I do in New Orleans who exhibit selflessness and strength that is truly heroic and holy—who absolutely look out for one another no matter their individual scarcity and pool everything they have.

We are fully awakening to something I did not even know existed when I opened my eyes in Villa Foyer in the early morning hours of 9/11. I believe it is God's utter unrestricted freedom to create us all anew by sharing his own life through us for the sake of others.

As Rowan Williams has preached:

> Jesus goes into the fertile darkness of death and his life broken open comes out of that darkness to be the life of his friends and the life of the world; life and light in abundance. The foundation of everything Christians try to do is in that process. The life of faith is about being broken open so that life may happen, relating to Jesus not as a distant figure setting a good example but as someone whose light and fire is kindled in us, so that for the world to see us who believe and struggle is to see *Jesus* . . . Christians are Christians because we sense that God's own life, broken, shared and buried has proven to be uncontainable.

This is who I understand awakened Americans to be: people who are beginning to live by grace God's own uncontainable life. Given God's unrestricted freedom we are of every race and faith tradition. We have taken note of the recent reminders that our days are not guaranteed and have made a conscious decision to live like we are dying—with that kind of fire and light. That means being willing to give up safety and enter difficult places. We can only do so because of who God has freed us to be, and for that grace we are eternally grateful.

As we write the next chapters of this story together we know there is another national narrative unfolding in America—not the war story but a spiritual narrative about the way God is entering our lives and waking us up to his compassion. In the extraordinary acts of self-sacrifice, the unprecedented acts of collective generosity, the sanctification of suffering, the large-scale awakening to a sense of shared fate, the mobilization of millions of volunteers—many in their teens and twenties—we see a glimpse of the conversion of life of which we all are capable, and the fire of God's own life which can and is bringing all of us into his eternal joy.

# JOIN THE AMERICAN AWAKENING

**www.anamericanawakening.com**

A network of newly awakened Americans, cracked open spiritually by our encounter with violent mortality, and responding with courage and growing commitment to live compassionately without reservation.

- Join an interactive social network of awakened Americans defining a new age of compassion and hope.
- Write the next chapters of *An American Awakening* by telling us your story of sacred activism.
- Organize peer-to-peer to create The Beloved Community.
- Log on to discuss faith and values.
- Add the voices of awakened Americans in your community to this growing switchboard for the liberation of the human spirit.
- Connect to the movement to build a new New Orleans and a new America.

**Tribute Center Walking Tours www.tributewtc.org**

Daily tours are conducted by guides drawn from the September 11th community including survivors, Lower Manhattan residents, recovery workers, volunteers who assisted in the recovery, and family members. Hear from figures in this story like Tony Palmeri whose lives were profoundly changed. Each tour is unique, weaving history and facts with personal experiences of survival, loss, and healing. Tours begin at 120 Liberty Street and last approximately an hour and fifteen minutes. Members of the September 11th community who would like to volunteer as tour guides are encouraged to contact the Tribute Center.

## www.odr.edola.org

The Office of Disaster Response of the Episcopal Diocese of Louisiana. The Mission of the Office of Disaster Response is to bring our hurricane-displaced neighbors home and to reclaim for all a dignified place in the building of a beloved community. The ODR provides meaningful work opportunities for spiritual growth to the many volunteers seeking to expand their capacity for generosity and selfless service. Volunteer for one of Katie Mears's rebuilding crews. Help build a Jericho house. Join Shakoor, Big Shed, and the youth of New Orleans in the Non-Violence Or Non-Existence campaign and much more.

## www.jerichohousing.org

Jericho Road is working with other nonprofits, private businesses, governmental agencies, and faith-based groups to create long-term housing strategies, unlocking underutilized land, rebuilding neighborhoods, and transforming communities in one of America's most culturally important cities. Log on to find out how you can help.

## www.actnola.org

All Congregations Together is a congregation-based community organization dedicated to empowering people to effect change and improve the quality of life for our families and communities in Greater New Orleans. ACT does this by working to develop leaders in its member congregations and by teaching them congregation-based organizing. Its members are united by faith—faith that teaches us to reach out to our neighbors; a faith that tells us that we have a responsibility to ease the suffering of our brothers and sisters, and leave this world knowing that because of us the world is a better place than it was when we entered it—that we have indeed made a difference.

## www.louisianajusticeinstitute.org

A nonprofit legal advocacy organization, LJI is responsive to a specific and urgent need for legal advocacy on behalf of impoverished communities and communities of color. LJI believes that a community-shared vision for social justice, combined with the opportunity and resolve to bring lasting change, will produce genuine equitable recovery in Louisiana. Plug into the civil rights initiatives being led by attorney Tracie Washington.

## www.equityandinclusion.org

The Equity and Inclusion Campaign is a policy advocacy and public messaging campaign advocating for fulfillment of the federal commitment to confront persistent poverty and inequity in the course of the Gulf Coast recovery. Their strategic allies combine voices and coordinate their efforts to influence the U.S. Congress and the executive branch so that historically disenfranchised groups have the political resources necessary to improve their lives and rebuild communities.

## www.algebra.org

The Algebra Project, Inc. is a 501(c)(3) national, nonprofit organization that uses mathematics as an organizing tool to ensure quality public school education for every child in America. We believe that every child has a right to a quality education to succeed in this technology-based society and to exercise full citizenship. We achieve this by using the best educational research and practices, and building coalitions to create systemic change.

## www.therethinkers.com

The Rethinkers are a group of students in New Orleans who want to rethink and rebuild our schools after Hurricane Katrina. Their vision is simple: a great education for every kid in our city, no matter the color of their skin, what neighborhood they stay in, or how much money their parents make. No one deserves a voice in rebuilding New Orleans schools more than the students who go to these places every single day.

## www.thechildrensdefense.org

The Children's Defense Fund has worked for thirty-five years to ensure a level playing field for all children. CDF implements public policy and promotes successful programs that lift children out of poverty, protect them from abuse and neglect, and provide a moral and spiritual foundation to help children succeed.

**www.myccra.org**

The Central City Renaissance Alliance is the organization leading the implementation of an exciting redevelopment plan created by Central City residents and people that work and worship in this historic neighborhood. Together we are revitalizing and redeveloping a vibrant community in the heart of New Orleans.